# Cotton Theory® Quilting 2

## Traditional Blocks

## Book Two
### Cotton Theory Series

# Betty Cotton

### Cotton Theory®
QUILTING

Cotton Theory, LLC
Osseo, Wisconsin

# Cotton Theory Quilting 2

Copyright © 2008 by Betty Cotton
All rights reserved. Published 2008
First Edition
16 15 14 13 12 11 10 09 08    1 2 3 4 5 6 7 8 9

Cotton Theory U.S. Patent No. 6,696,129

This book was produced and published by Cotton Theory, LLC

P.O. Box 22            Phone: (715) 597-2883 or (800) 673-8075
13900 7th Street      E-mail: quiltyard@quiltyard.com
Osseo, WI 54758       Internet: www.quiltyard.com

We welcome your suggestions and comments.

**Publisher:** Betty Cotton/Cotton Theory, LLC
**Project assistants:** Nancy Eichel, Donna Hanson, Loretta Jarocki, Betty Nyseth,
Betty Slezak, Sue Wilson, Katie Wolff
**Editor:** Monica Stauber Holtz
**Book designers:** Andrew Clausen, Monica Stauber Holtz
**Technical illustrators:** Andrew Clausen, Betty Cotton
**Cover photographer:** Shane Opatz
**Room and project photographers:** R.G., Shane Opatz

Embroidery designs by Pfaff, Anita Goodesigns, Cactus Punch, Oklahoma Embroidery Supply & Design,
and Colonial Patterns (Aunt Martha's Hot Iron Transfers) are used in this book with permission.

Portions of this book have been previously published in slightly different form in
*Cotton Theory Quilting: Quilt First–Then Assemble*, copyright © 2006 by Betty Cotton

ISBN-13:  978-0-9772611-1-6
ISBN-10:  0-9772611-1-5

Library of Congress Control Number: 2008922449

Printed in the United States of America

# Dedication

**To Sue Wilson**

A retired schoolteacher, Sue puts in more hours keeping pace
with me than she did teaching school. I am very grateful
Sue retired, because now she devotes almost every minute of
every day to Cotton Theory quilting.

# Acknowledgments

A very special thank you to all of the certified Cotton Theory instructors whose
positive feedback, support, advice, and enjoyment of Cotton Theory quilting
inspired me to create more designs.

**Special thanks and appreciation go to the following individuals:**

My husband and business partner, Jack Cotton, who has tolerated tantrums and
tears, along with a house that feels like Grand Central Station.

My daughters, Sarah and Katie,
for keeping me on track with all of the deadlines.

Nancy Eichel, Donna Hanson, Loretta Jarocki, Betty Nyseth,
Betty Slezak, Sue Wilson, and Katie Wolff for contributing their time constructing
quilts and testing new techniques.

My publishing assistant, Monica Holtz, who has combed through my ill-written
proofs. Her advice has been so valuable in the past that I am forever grateful to
have her in the present, and my goal is to have her in the future as well.

Betty Cotton

# Contents

# Part Three – Cotton Theory Projects

Skill Level

# Part Four – Finishing Up

# Cotton Theory® Quilting Using Traditional Blocks

Quilt First – Then Assemble™ is the motto of Cotton Theory quilting, and it's as easy as it sounds. You simply "quilt as you go."

With traditional quilts, the actual quilting process is often the least favorite part of constructing a quilt, especially if the project is large. But with Cotton Theory quilting, the process becomes enjoyable. Pieces are layered with batting, quilted individually, and then sewn together.

Imagine connecting tiny quilts into one big, completely reversible quilt. That's what Cotton Theory quilting is all about. Large seam allowances are folded and topstitched into place on the outside of the quilt, adding an eye-catching, three-dimensional look to the finished project.

Cotton Theory quilting methods can be used with traditional quilt blocks if simple modifications are made. Although traditional quilt blocks do not have large seam allowances, extra fabric can be cleverly incorporated to solve this problem.

**To create a reversible Cotton Theory quilt, traditional blocks are layered with batting and quilted before they are joined together with large seam allowances. Folding and topstitching the seam allowances on the outside of the quilt adds an extra dimension to Cotton Theory projects.**

This book shows you how to enlarge back-side fabrics, reduce overall dimensions of blocks, and use setting triangles and framing strips to construct Cotton Theory quilts with traditional blocks.

If you have acquired quilt blocks from relatives, block-of-the-month programs, block exchanges, or other sources, now is the time to turn them into finished quilts. Although most projects in this book include instructions for piecing blocks, you can substitute your own blocks and skip the associated yardage, cutting, and piecing for those blocks. Instructions in each chapter explain how to cut, layer, quilt, and assemble projects. You can quilt your blocks as desired and assemble your own unique Cotton Theory quilt.

You can use decorative stitches, contrasting thread colors, embroidery, bobbin work, folding techniques, and bindings to produce the quilt of your dreams. All you need are fabric, sewing supplies, your sewing machine, and your imagination.

# Part One
# Getting Ready

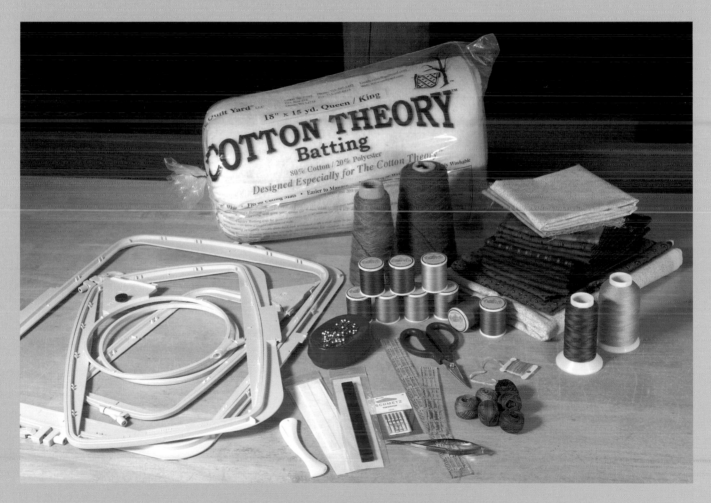

Start each project with the right sewing,
quilting, and embroidery supplies.

# Supplies

## Fabric

❖ Good quality fabric is essential.

❖ Select fabrics of compatible weight for each project.

❖ Choose lightweight, 100 percent cotton fabrics for quilts and quilt-like projects.

❖ Choose medium-weight, 100 percent cotton fabrics for area rugs and floor quilts.

## Batting

❖ Cotton Theory Batting is 80 percent cotton, 20 percent polyester, and is perfect for all Cotton Theory projects. Because this batting is only 18 inches wide, it fits on cutting mats. It is completely washable, has no wrinkles or creases, and has very little shrinkage (3 percent). When pressed with a hot steam iron, the 20 percent polyester in the batting lightly adheres to cotton fabrics, temporarily holding them together and eliminating pinning. The batting will become half the thickness when pressed with hot steam, giving projects drapeability. Cotton Theory Batting can be ordered on the Internet at www.quiltyard. com or by phoning (715) 597-2883 or (800) 673-8075.

**Cotton Theory Batting**

## Cutting Tools and Equipment

❖ **Cutting table** – A 36-inch high cutting surface is comfortable for most people to use while standing.

❖ **Rotary cutters** – Use a 45 mm cutter for lightweight fabric and a 60 mm cutter for batting. Cover the blade when the cutter is not in use.

❖ **Acrylic rulers** – Use a 5" x 24" ruler for fabric, a 4" x 36" ruler for batting, a 1" x 12" ruler for measuring placement of a quilting guide or seam gauge, and a 12" x 12" ruler for squaring up corners. The rulers should have ⅛-inch, ¼-inch, and 45-degree marks.

❖ **Self-healing cutting mat** – A 24" x 36" mat works well for fabric and batting. Markings for ⅛-inch increments and 45 degrees are helpful.

- ❖ **Scissors** – You'll need sharp scissors that can cut through several layers of fabric, a small thread snips to cut threads, and a seam ripper to remove stitches. Cotton Theory Scissors have short, sharp blades and large, easy-to-grip handles that allow you to cut bulky layers with precision. These scissors can be ordered on the Internet at www.quiltyard.com or by calling (715) 597-2883 or (800) 673-8075.

Cotton Theory Scissors

## Marking Tools

- ❖ **Hera marker** – This small plastic tool has a sharp edge that allows you to make temporary crease marks on fabric.

- ❖ **Chalk** – If you prefer chalk, use yellow marking chalk on dark-colored fabric and blue marking chalk on light-colored fabric. Test the chalk on scrap fabric to make sure it is safe to use on your project.

## Sewing Tools

- ❖ **Sewing machine and accessories** – A straight stitch and zigzag stitch are required. Decorative stitches and an embroidery unit are optional.

  A ¼-inch presser foot is helpful for accurate piecing of traditional blocks. This presser foot allows you to sew ¼-inch seam allowances easily.

  A walking foot is extremely beneficial. It evenly feeds layers when you're quilting by machine.

- ❖ **Cotton Theory Adhesive Quilting Guide** – When used on your sewing machine, this adhesive tool helps you guide the raw edges of your fabric to produce accurate quilting and precise seam allowances.

  The Cotton Theory Adhesive Quilting Guide can be ordered on the Internet at www.quiltyard.com or by calling (715) 597-2883 or (800) 673-8075. Adhesive refills for the guide also are available.

- ❖ **Bobbins** – Keep a minimum of four to six bobbins on hand for small projects and 10 to 12 for large projects.

- ❖ **Cone holder** – This holds large spools or 2,000-yard to 3,000-yard cones of thread.

- ❖ **Thread** – You can use a variety of weights and brands in solid as well as variegated colors. Different threads will create different effects on the front side and back side of your project.

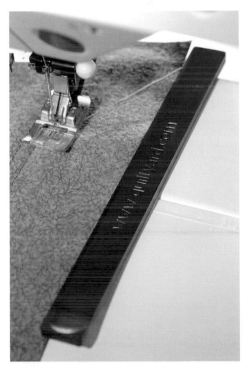

Cotton Theory Adhesive Quilting Guide

King Tut 40-weight variegated cotton thread, manufactured by Superior Threads, works well on the top of your sewing machine for all aspects of Cotton Theory projects, including piecing, quilting, assembly, topstitching, embroidery, and binding. It also can be used in the bobbin, but the bobbin tension may need to be adjusted.

Betty Cotton's Cottage Colors collection of King Tut thread can be ordered on the Internet at www.quiltyard.com or by calling (715) 597-2883 or (800) 673-8075.

**Betty Cotton's Cottage Colors collection of King Tut thread**

Good quality 50-weight cotton thread also is an appropriate choice for Cotton Theory quilting. It can be used on the top of your machine and in the bobbin.

You usually can use 30-weight, 40-weight, or 50-weight cotton thread on the top and 50-weight cotton thread in the bobbin without adjusting the bobbin tension.

Choose specialty threads, such as metallic, rayon, and some blends, if you want to change the look of your work or emphasize a certain area when quilting.

Threads that are too heavy to fit through the eye of a sewing machine needle can be wound on a bobbin and used for quilting. For this type of bobbin work, you must loosen the bobbin tension to compensate for the thickness of the thread.

❖ **Machine needles** – Different sewing machine needles usually are needed for different tasks. When sewing with 50-weight cotton thread, choose the following:

For piecing, use size 80/12 or 70/10 universal needles.

For quilting, use size 90/14 or 80/12 quilting needles.

For embroidery, use size 90/14 titanium embroidery needles.

For topstitching, use size 90/14 topstitch needles.

When sewing with King Tut 40-weight cotton, a size 90/14 topstitch needle can be used for all of the above tasks.

Keep a supply of needles on hand; they will dull quickly.

❖ **Hand needle** – Use a sharp, No. 11 needle for tacking mitered corners of binding.

❖ **Straight pins and holder** – Use thin and sharp straight pins with glass heads. A magnetic straight pin holder works best to keep pins where they belong when they're not in use.

If you prefer, you can use wash-away, double-sided, ¼-inch tape to eliminate pinning.

❖ **Tape measure** – Choose one that measures 120 inches.

❖ **Lint brush** – A good-quality, ½-inch brush, such as an artist's brush, is ideal for cleaning the bobbin case and presser bar of your sewing machine. Use it often.

## Pressing Tools

❖ **Iron** – For best results, use a heavyweight, self-cleaning iron that produces heavy steam and has small holes in the bottom plate.

❖ **Ironing board** – You'll need an ironing board or other large, padded surface, such as a "big board," to press your pieces. A "big board" is a large board that fits on top of your ironing board and has its own cover.

❖ **Spring water** – Use bottled spring water to fill your iron and create steam. Spring water is free of added chemicals.

## Embroidery Tools

If you plan to do quilted embroidery, you'll need the following tools:

❖ **Embroidery machine or a sewing machine with an embroidery unit**.

❖ **Embroidery designs** – Outline designs work best.

❖ **Embroidery needles** – Size 90/14 titanium machine embroidery needles work well.

**Use outline designs for quilted embroidery.**

❖ **Water-soluble stabilizer** – The stabilizer helps hold fabric during machine embroidery, and it rinses away when the fabric is washed.

❖ **Embroidery hoops** – It's best to have a variety of sizes to accommodate different projects.

❖ **Thread** – You can use a variety of weights and brands.

❖ **Bobbins** – Do not use prewound bobbins. Fill bobbins with good-quality thread.

❖ **Embroidery scissors** – A 4-inch to 5-inch machine embroidery scissors is useful.

## Other Tools

❖ **Swing-arm lamp** – This type of lamp allows you to put direct light where you want it when you are layering, pinning, quilting, sewing, folding, and topstitching.

❖ **Adjustable chair** – For greatest comfort and support while sewing and quilting, use a chair that's adjustable.

❖ **Spray sizing** – Use sizing to make ironing easier without added stiffness.

❖ **Sliding seam gauge** – This 6-inch ruler with a slide mechanism allows you to lock in a specific measurement.

# Words to Know

**Aligning intersections** – Lining up seams of quilt connectors while assembling a Cotton Theory quilt, even though these seams do not touch each other. Aligning the intersections gives a quilt a professionally finished appearance.

**Back side** – When selecting fabric for a reversible quilt, this is the right side of the back fabric.

**Back sides together** – Placing reversible quilted pieces against each other back side to back side, with right sides of the back fabrics touching, when assembling a Cotton Theory quilt.

**Baste** – To secure layers together temporarily with long stitches for easy removal.

**Batting** – A layer of material between front-side and back-side fabrics that adds dimension and warmth to quilt projects.

**Bias** – The diagonal of woven fabric, generally a 45-degree angle to any straight edge. This angle provides the most stretch. (See Fabric Diagram 1 at bottom of page.)

**Bias binding** – Binding made from fabric squares that have been cut on the bias and then sewn together into a long strip. Plaid fabrics are commonly used for bias binding, because the angle of the fabric's color bars makes the binding especially attractive.

**Binding** – The finished edge of a quilt, consisting of a continuous strip of fabric sewn onto the back side of the quilt and then folded over to the front side, where it is sewn in place by machine.

**Block shrinkage** – Decrease in the size of a traditional quilt block when large seam allowances are used to construct a Cotton Theory project. The large seam allowances cause a traditional block to shrink by as much as 1 inch on each of its four sides.

**Bobbin work** – The use of heavy threads, ribbon, floss, and yarn that are too thick to fit in the eye of a sewing machine needle. These are wound on bobbins and used for quilting.

**Borders** – Quilted pieces attached to the outer edges of a section or project to enlarge it.

**Chain quilting** – Continuously feeding quilt pieces under the presser foot of a sewing machine one after the other. This speeds up quilting and creates a chain of pieces that are later separated by snipping a few threads.

**Channel** – The space between two parallel rows of stitching.

**Channel quilting** – Quilting done in a series of lines that are spaced evenly apart, creating channels.

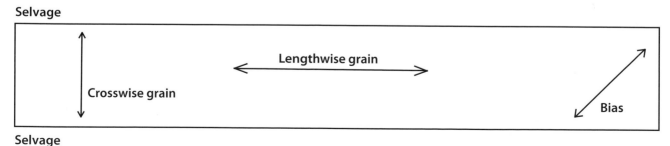

**Fabric Diagram 1**

**Connector (or sashing)** – The quilted piece that connects blocks, rows, or sections of a quilt.

**Corner posts** – Quilt pieces that serve as intersections for connectors or as corner units that join borders of a quilt.

**Cotton Theory seam** – A seam consisting of enlarged seam allowances folded and stitched on the outside of a Cotton Theory quilt, creating an extra dimension in the fabric.

**Crosswise grain** – The direction of woven fabric that runs selvage to selvage. (See Fabric Diagram 1 on previous page.)

**Decorative stitch** – Any stitch other than a straight stitch.

**Directional stitch** – Any stitch that extends only in one direction, either to the right or to the left, when it is sewn. Blanket stitches and hem stitches are examples of directional stitches.

**Double-fold** – Folding fabric twice. Generally the fabric is folded ¼ inch from its edge and then is folded over ⅜ inch again.

**Embroidery** – A design stitched by hand or by machine on fabric layers that have been placed in a hoop to keep the fabric from puckering.

**Embroidery hoop** – A circular, square, or rectangular framing device that holds layers securely for hand or machine embroidery.

**Enlarged back-side blocks** – Back-side pieces that are cut larger than front-side traditional quilt blocks to accommodate the large seam allowances needed for Cotton Theory quilting.

**Extra dimension** – Added thickness and depth created when Cotton Theory seam allowances are folded and finished on the outside of the quilt.

**Fat eighth** – A quarter of a yard of fabric that is opened to its full width and cut in half parallel to the selvages. This creates an eighth of a yard that is fatter than standard. With fabric that is 42 inches wide, a fat eighth is 9" x 21", and a standard eighth is 4½" x 42".

**Fat quarter** – One-half yard of fabric that is opened to its full width and cut in half parallel to the selvages. This creates a quarter of a yard that is fatter than standard. With fabric that is 42 inches wide, a fat quarter is 18" x 21", and a standard quarter is 9" x 42".

**Framing strip** – A fabric strip added to a quilt block to enlarge it. The strip is sewn to the block with a ¼-inch seam.

**Freeway™ procedure** – Finishing a seam on the outside of a project by pressing seam allowances open and double-folding one side out and under, then double-folding the other side up and in toward the middle, before stitching each into place. The outward fold allows fabric from the opposite side of the quilt to show through, adding extra color and giving the illusion of a very narrow border.

**Front side** – When selecting fabric for a reversible quilt, this is the right side of the front fabric.

**Half-square triangle** – Triangle created by dividing a square in half diagonally. Cotton Theory projects often include two fabric squares that make half-square triangles when joined together.

**Highway™ procedure** – Finishing seams on the outside of a project by pressing seam allowances open and then double-folding both sides toward the middle before stitching them into place. This gives the appearance of a highway that has two lanes.

**Joining stitch** – Any stitch that extends left and right with equal width measurements, often joining two sides. Such stitches include the zigzag, bridging stitch, feather stitch, and herringbone.

**Label** – Information about a quilt and its maker that is stitched to or stitched in the finished project.

**Layering** – Placing batting between the wrong sides of front-side fabric and back-side fabric.

**Lengthwise grain** – The direction of woven fabric that runs parallel to the selvage. (See Fabric Diagram 1 on Page 12.)

**Merging Lanes™ procedure** – A quilt construction where two Cotton Theory One-Way Street seams are so close together that the folds touch each other. This gives the appearance of a Cotton Theory Highway seam without topstitching down the middle.

**Mitered corner** – A seam sewn diagonally where two outside edges meet to form a corner, such as on a cloth napkin.

**Mitered seam** – A seam sewn diagonally on the bias when two fabric pieces are placed right sides together.

**One-Way Street™ procedure** – Finishing seams on the outside of a project by pressing seam allowances all to one side, trimming one or more seam allowances, and then double-folding the remaining seam allowances before stitching them into place. This gives the appearance of a one-way street that has only one lane.

**Overpass™ procedure** – Pinching together and bar-tacking the folded edges of a Cotton Theory Highway seam to add a lift and an extra dimension to a project.

**Piecing** – Joining two fabric pieces, right sides together, with a ¼-inch seam.

**Press** – Using an iron on a cotton or linen setting to adhere front fabric, batting, and back fabric together with steam. Pressing means lifting up and setting down the iron. The iron should not be rocked or pushed side to side.

**Presser-foot width** – The width between the needle and outside edge of the presser foot on a sewing machine.

**Quilt blocks** – Units made by sewing fabric pieces together with a ¼-inch seam to create a design. The blocks, which are often square or rectangular and can be many different sizes, are joined together to construct a quilt.

**Quilting** – The process of sewing together at least three layers of materials.

**Reversible binding** – Two different fabrics pieced together along their long edges to give a reversible quilt compatible fabric binding that matches each side.

**Reversible quilt** – A quilt constructed so that the back side looks as good as the front, providing two equal quilts in one.

**Right sides together** – Placing two fabrics or fabric sections together with their brighter sides, or right sides, against each other.

**Sashing (or connector)** – The quilted piece that connects blocks, rows, or sections of a quilt.

**Scrappy** – A mixture of colors and prints with no prearranged order.

**Seam allowance** – The distance between cut edges of fabric and the seam. The seam allowance is created by stitching together two fabric pieces. The allowance usually is ¼ inch from the cut edge for traditional piecing and 1 inch or more from the cut edge for Cotton Theory projects.

**Selvage** – The manufactured, tightly woven, narrow edge of fabric that prevents the cloth from raveling. Selvage edges should be removed and should not be used in quilt projects.

**Setting triangles** – Triangles added to all four sides of a quilt block, therefore enlarging it and turning it on point (with corners pointing up/down and left/right).

**Skill level** – Identification of a person's skill, ranging from beginner to expert.

**Stitch in the ditch** – To stitch on an existing seam line. In Cotton Theory quilting, this stitching will be visible on one or both sides of the quilt and will not be hidden.

**Stitch length** – The distance between stitch links, measured in a metric scale. The higher the number, the longer the stitch. A stitch length of 3.5 mm is ideal for quilt assembly.

**Stitch width** – The distance from one side of a stitch to the other side, measured in a metric scale. The higher the number, the wider the stitch.

**Strip** – A piece of fabric cut from selvage to selvage (crosswise grain). (See Fabric Diagram 2 at bottom of page.)

**Sub-cut** – A second cut (lengthwise grain) taken from the original cut strip. (See Fabric Diagram 3 at bottom of page.)

**Tension** – The interlocking of the top thread and bobbin thread on a sewing machine. With the correct tension, thread should interlock midway between fabric layers so that stitches lie flat and fabric does not pucker.

**Topstitching** – Functional or decorative stitching sewn over a fold or seam.

**Wobble stitch** – A zigzag stitch altered in width and length to resemble hand quilting, looking a little wobbly.

**Wrong side** – The dull side, or inside surface, of fabric. Usually this side is not intended to be seen in a completed project.

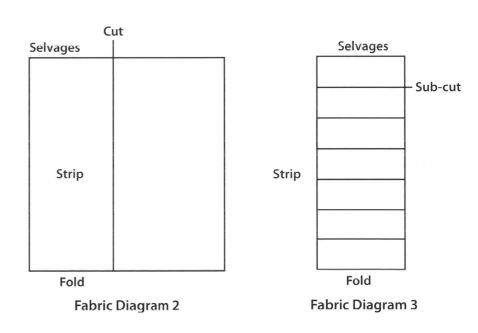

Fabric Diagram 2            Fabric Diagram 3

# Part Two
# The Basics

**After pieces are layered, they're ready for quilting.**

# Preparation

## Fabric Selection

Because Cotton Theory quilts are reversible, you will need fabrics and similar amounts of yardage for both sides of the quilt. You will cut pieces for both the front side and back side.

Selecting fabric for projects in this book is fairly easy. You can use your own quilt blocks to start a project or you can piece together blocks by following instructions in the chapters.

Here is some advice on fabric and color selection:

**Cotton Theory projects are reversible.**

❖ If you use your own blocks, you can choose colors from those blocks for the connectors, borders, and other pieces you will need to complete the quilt.

❖ If you decide to piece together blocks in a project, but you change the colors, you should choose colors of a similar value so you can preserve the overall look of the quilt. For instance, if olive green and dark purple are listed for a block, you could replace them with rust and navy blue to produce the same contrast. Replace dark colors with dark colors, medium colors with medium colors, and light colors with light colors.

❖ Using a color wheel can help you select fabrics, too. Color wheels can be found at many quilt shops, art supply stores, and on the Internet. They show primary and intermediate colors in a circular diagram. Related colors are next to each other and complementary colors are opposite each other on the wheel. Complementary colors add appealing contrast to a quilt. Red and green are complementary colors, for instance, and they appeal to almost everyone. Blue and orange, as well as yellow and violet, also are complementary colors. Whether you are looking for the perfect contrasting colors or are comparing hues for back-side and front-side fabrics, a color wheel can provide answers.

## Fabric Preparation

It's a good idea to preshrink fabric before cutting and sewing. Washing and drying will preshrink fabric and remove excess dye and sizing. Batting will automatically shrink with the pressing of a hot steam iron. Quilters who prefer not to prewash fabric should expect bleeding of dyes and some shrinkage if a quilt project is washed. The decision to prewash fabric is up to the quilter and may depend on the type of project.

# Cutting

Cutting fabric and batting for Cotton Theory projects differs from that of traditionally constructed projects. Fabric pieces must be cut for the front side and back side of each quilt, and batting pieces must be cut, too.

❖ When possible, cut front-side and back-side fabric pieces together. This eliminates pairing them up later.

❖ Label your cut pieces for the front side, back side and batting to avoid confusion during construction of your project. Pin or tape labels to these pieces.

❖ Remember that the lengthwise grain of fabric is less likely to stretch than the crosswise grain, so whenever possible, folded seam allowances should be the lengthwise grain. This will eliminate the possibility of wavy seam allowances, and your quilted pieces will remain their true size.

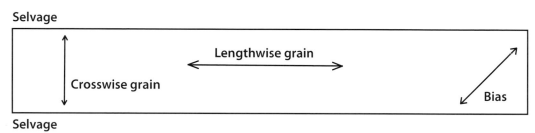

**Example:** Cut one 10-inch strip of fabric from the fold to selvages (crosswise grain), and then sub-cut eight 4" x 10" pieces from that strip (lengthwise grain), as shown in the illustrations below.

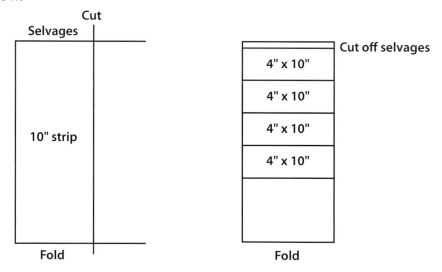

❖ Like fabric, batting also is cut piece by piece. Specific batting cutting instructions are provided with each Cotton Theory project. Batting pieces will be smaller than fabric pieces.

## Thread Selection

Your fabrics determine what thread you choose. In a traditional quilt, thread usually matches or blends with the back-side fabric. But because Cotton Theory quilts are reversible, you need to choose threads for both sides of the quilt. You can have one color of thread in your bobbin and a totally different color in the top part of your sewing machine.

Following are some thread selection tips:

❖ Use good quality thread in the bobbin and on the top of your sewing machine for all aspects of Cotton Theory quilting, including machine embroidery. Avoid lesser quality thread that is sometimes used in bobbins for machine embroidery. With Cotton Theory quilting, it is important that the back side of your project look as good as the front.

❖ For busy prints, match the thread to your fabric.

❖ For simple prints and plain fabrics, use a contrasting thread color.

❖ Choose from a variety of thread weights and brands in solid or variegated colors, depending on your preferences and your particular projects. Cotton thread is an excellent choice in both 50-weight (regular utility weight) and 40-weight (a bit heavier). King Tut 40-weight cotton was used in all of the Cotton Theory projects in this book. This high quality thread, manufactured by Superior Threads, handles quilting, embroidery, piecing and topstitching with ease. If you use King Tut thread in your bobbin, you may need to adjust the bobbin tension. Otherwise, use 50-weight cotton in the bobbin.

❖ Different weights of thread require different sizes of sewing machine needles. The charts below show requirements for 50-weight cotton and for King Tut 40-weight cotton. Please note that King Tut thread needs only one type of needle for several different types of tasks.

### 50-weight thread and needles
**Top thread:** 50-weight cotton
**Bobbin thread:** 50-weight cotton
**Piecing:** size 80/12 or 70/10 universal needle
**Quilting:** size 90/14 or 80/12 quilting needle
**Embroidery:** size 90/14 titanium embroidery needle
**Topstitching:** size 90/14 topstitch needle

### King Tut thread and needle
**Top thread:** King Tut 40-weight variegated cotton
**Bobbin thread:** 50-weight cotton
**Piecing:** size 90/14 topstitch needle
**Quilting:** size 90/14 topstitch needle
**Embroidery:** size 90/14 topstitch needle
**Topstitching:** size 90/14 topstitch needle

## Layering

To prepare Cotton Theory projects for quilting, you need to make small quilt sandwiches by layering fabric pieces and batting together.

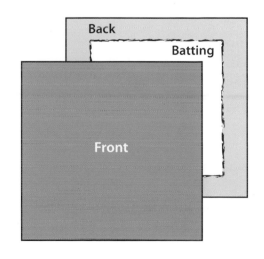

❖ Place the back fabric piece right side down, place the batting piece on the back fabric, and then place the front fabric piece on top of the batting right side up.

Batting usually is centered on the back fabric during layering, but some situations call for batting to be aligned with one or more raw edges. Specific instructions in each Cotton Theory project chapter explain the correct layering. Because batting is not included in the seam allowances of Cotton Theory projects, the batting will be smaller than the fabric.

❖ Press layered pieces with steam to secure them for quilting. The 20 percent polyester content of Cotton Theory Batting temporarily adheres the layers together when pressed, eliminating the need for pinning. Large or especially long pieces still may require some pins to keep layers in place.

Pressing reduces the loft of Cotton Theory Batting, but when the completed project is tumbled in the dryer, the loft returns, and details in the quilt become more noticeable.

## Quilting

There are numerous ways to quilt layered pieces. You're limited only by your imagination and your sewing machine. Project chapters gives quilting suggestions, but you can change these to suit your preferences. Because you're working with small layered pieces, quilting becomes easy.

❖ Decorative stitches, embroidered outlines, and the "upside down" stitches of bobbin work can be used to quilt pieces beautifully. A favorite quilting stitch for Cotton Theory projects is the "wobble," a zigzag altered so it is very narrow and appears a little wobbly, like hand quilting. Instructions for all of these quilting methods are included in various projects in this book.

❖ For plain fabrics and simple prints, use decorative stitches and contrasting thread to add appealing details to your quilt.

❖ For busy prints, use the wobble stitch or a straight stitch to quilt rows across the fabric, and match thread to the fabric.

After all of your pieces are quilted, they're ready to be assembled into a Cotton Theory table runner, wall hanging, bed quilt, or other project. Unlike traditional quilts, there's no need to add backing, because the backing is already there. All you have to do is sew your quilted pieces together to produce a reversible quilt. Assembly techniques are described in the next chapter.

**This Line Dance Runner was quilted piece by piece and then assembled using Cotton Theory techniques. Step-by-step instructions are in the projects section of this book.**

# Techniques

Assembling a Cotton Theory quilt with traditional blocks involves techniques that are different from traditional quilting. Instead of a ¼-inch seam allowance, Cotton Theory techniques require a minimum 1-inch seam allowance when sewing one quilted piece to another quilted piece. This enlarged seam allowance is finished on the outside of the quilt, adding an extra decorative dimension.

Because traditional blocks don't include a large seam allowance, special quilt settings and alterations are used to modify the blocks for Cotton Theory projects. These modifications are:

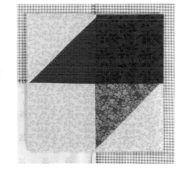

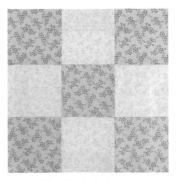

**Enlarged back-side block**

**Block shrinkage** (After assembly, block will be 1" smaller on all sides.)

❖ **Enlarged back-side blocks** – Back-side pieces that are cut larger than front-side traditional blocks to accommodate large seam allowances.

❖ **Block shrinkage** – A decrease in the size of a traditional block when large seam allowances are used.

❖ **Setting triangles** – Triangles added to all four sides of a traditional block to enlarge it.

❖ **Framing strips** – Fabric strips added to a quilt block to enlarge it.

After modifications have been made, traditional blocks easily can be assembled into Cotton Theory quilts.

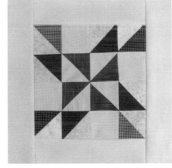

**Setting triangles**

**Framing strips**

Batting is layered between front-side and back-side fabric pieces, and then the layers are quilted, leaving raw fabric edges that are finished into a reversible quilt. There is no batting in the seam allowances, because this would cause too much bulk. The batting pieces usually measure 1 inch less than the fabric on all sides, except in special circumstances noted in Cotton Theory patterns.

Cotton Theory techniques include the Highway™, One-Way Street™, Freeway™, Overpass, and Merging Lanes procedures, a construction step called Aligned Intersections, and various types of quilting, bobbin work, and quilted embroidery.

# Highway™ Procedure

The Highway procedure is a great way to attach one quilted piece to another quilted piece whenever the pieces have no bulky seams. For bulky seamed pieces, use the One-Way Street procedure, described later in this chapter.

In the Highway procedure, two quilted pieces are sewn together with a minimum 1-inch seam allowance. Then

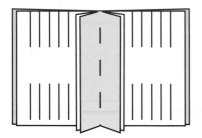

seam allowances are pressed open, with two layers of fabric on each side of the seam. (Cotton Theory seam allowances have a total of four layers of fabric – two from each quilted piece.)

Quilted pieces are ready to be joined using the Highway procedure.

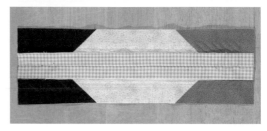

The pieces are sewn together, and seam allowances are pressed open.

## To finish a Highway seam:

❖ Press seam allowances open. It's best to press both sides of the project to ensure that seams are completely open and lie flat. Use a steam iron to press seams open; then flip the project over and press the other side.

❖ Double-fold each side of the seam allowance (two layers) toward the center, and pin it in place. To accomplish this, fold each side upward ¼ inch and then fold it again so it meets the seam line in the middle. Raw edges of the fabric are now tucked inside the folds.

Fold the seam allowance ¼ inch and then fold it again so it meets the seam line.

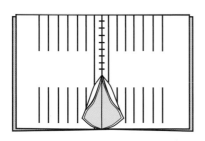

All pins should face the same direction so they can be removed easily while topstitching. If you prefer, you can eliminate pinning by using wash-away, double-sided, ¼-inch tape.

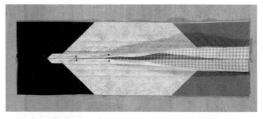

Double-fold and pin each side of the seam allowance.

❖ Topstitch the folds where the two sides meet. The stitch should be wide enough to sew both sides of the folded seam allowances at the same time. Topstitch through all layers. (See Stitches chapter for advice on choosing stitches.)

Next, topstitch the folds where the two sides meet.

# One-Way Street™ Procedure

The One-Way Street procedure has more flexibility than the Highway procedure. It allows you to cross over a previously folded and stitched seam.

After two quilted pieces are sewn together with a minimum 1-inch seam allowance, the seam allowances are pressed in one direction, with all layers together on one side of the seam. (Cotton Theory seam allowances have four layers – two from each quilted piece.) The seam allowance layers may be different sizes, with some smaller than others, depending on the specific quilting project.

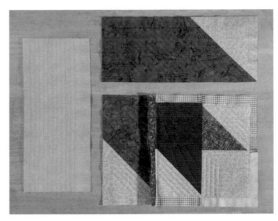

These quilted pieces will be joined together using the One-Way Street procedure. One seam on the pieces at the bottom of the photo is ready to be folded and topstitched.

### To finish a One-Way Street seam:

❖ Press all four seam allowances in one direction, as indicated in the instructions for each project. To ensure that seams are smooth and flat, use a steam iron to press the opposite side of the project first; then press the side that has seam allowances.

❖ Trim the top two layers of the seam allowances to ¼ inch. (When using a traditional quilt block, one layer already may be ¼ inch, so you only 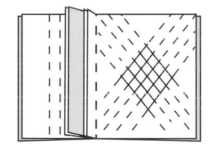 need to trim the second layer.) Do not cut the bottom two layers because these will be needed for folding and finishing.

When using a traditional quilt block, one layer of the One-Way Street seam allowance may already be ¼ inch, so you only need to trim the second layer before folding and topstitching the bottom two layers.

❖ Double-fold the bottom two layers back to the original seam line (not past it), and pin the fold in place. To accomplish this, make a ¼-inch fold and then fold again to the seam line. Raw edges of the fabric are now tucked inside the folds. Do not cover up the original seam line while folding; you need to barely see it so you can stitch on top of it. To make sewing and pin removal easier, position the fabric so

Fold the seam allowance ¼ inch, as shown above, and then fold it again, back to the original seam line, as shown below.

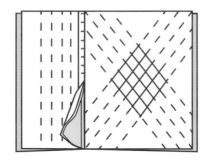

you fold seam allowances toward you if you pin fabric right-handed or away from you if you pin fabric left-handed. This will put straight pins in the proper direction for easy removal, and as the project gets larger, bulk will not build up in the throat of the sewing machine. If you prefer, you can eliminate pinning by using wash-away, double-sided, ¼-inch tape.

❖ Using a zigzag or decorative stitch of your choice, topstitch the folded fabric in place. To do this, stitch in the ditch (on the previous seam line), going on and off the fold. (See Stitches chapter for advice on choosing stitches.)

## Crossing over a seam:

The One-Way Street procedure is the best technique to use when attaching one quilted piece to another that already has a folded and finished seam. Follow the previous instructions for finishing a One-Way Street seam, but keep these points in mind:

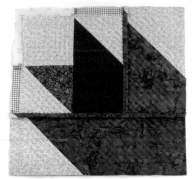

The One-Way Street procedure was used to connect the bottom quilted piece to the top piece that already had a finished seam.

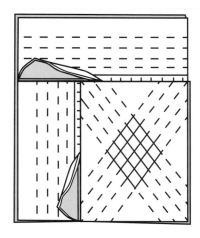

❖ Trim the old, and fold the new. In other words, press all seam allowances toward the new piece you added, so that the previously finished, intersecting seam can be seen on top. Then trim the top two seam allowance layers, including the intersecting seam, to ¼ inch or less to reduce the fabric bulk.

❖ After trimming, double-fold the bottom two seam allowance layers and topstitch by following the usual instructions for the One-Way Street procedure.

## Freeway™ Procedure

The Freeway procedure adds an extra color to a folded seam, making it look like a narrow border, even though it isn't. It's simply a different way of finishing Cotton Theory seam allowances.

Two quilted pieces are sewn together with a minimum 1-inch seam allowance, and the seam allowances are pressed open, just as they are in the Highway procedure. There should be two layers of seam allowance on each side of the seam. (Cotton Theory seam allowances have a total of four layers of fabric – two from each quilted piece.) Next, seam allowances on one side of the seam are double-folded out and under, away from the middle, and seam allowances on the other side are double-folded up and in toward the middle.

Fabric from the opposite side of the quilt is visible when

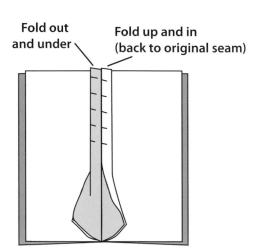

Fold out and under

Fold up and in (back to original seam)

the seam is pressed open, and this fabric remains visible when seam allowances are folded out and under. Color from the opposite side of the quilt shows through, adding an unexpected splash of something new.

### To finish a Freeway seam:

❖ Press seam allowances open with a steam iron. To ensure that seams are completely open and lie flat, flip the project over and press that side, too.

❖ Double-fold one side of the seam allowance (two layers) out and under, and pin it in place. To accomplish this, make a ¼-inch fold and then fold again, usually lining up the folded edge along a row of quilting. (In some cases, there may not be a row of quilting near the fold.) Raw edges of the fabric are now tucked inside the folds. All pins should face the same direction so they can be removed easily while topstitching. If you prefer, you can eliminate pinning by using wash-away, double-sided, ¼-inch tape.

Double-fold one side of the seam allowance out and under.

❖ Using a zigzag or decorative stitch, topstitch the folded fabric in place, going on and off the fold and sewing on top of the row of quilting by the folded edge. (See Stitches chapter for advice on choosing stitches.)

❖ Double-fold the other side of the seam allowance up and in toward the middle, back to the original seam line, and pin it in place. This side should be folded ¼ inch and then folded again so it meets the seam line. Raw edges of the fabric are now tucked inside the folds. All pins should face the same direction.

After one folded side is topstitched, as shown on the left, the remaining seam allowances are double-folded back to the original seam and are topstitched, as shown on the right.

❖ Using the same zigzag or decorative stitch as before, topstitch the folded fabric in place, sewing across the middle line where the two fabrics meet, just as you would in the Highway procedure.

## Merging Lanes™ Procedure

When assembling a Cotton Theory quilt with connectors that finish at ¾" between blocks, the folds of the One-Way Street seams are so close together that they touch each other. This is called the Merging Lanes procedure. This construction looks like a Highway seam without any stitching down the middle.

The connector joining these blocks is one example of the Merging Lanes procedure.

## Overpass™ Procedure

The Overpass procedure is a modified version of the Highway procedure. To add an extra dimension, or lift, to the finished folds of a Highway seam, simply pinch the folds together and bar-tack them. Bar-tacking means stitching in place with a small width, such as a zigzag altered to 2.0 mm wide and 0.0 mm long.

The design of each Cotton Theory project determines whether the Overpass procedure will be a good addition to the quilt.

The Overpass procedure will give your quilt an extra dimension. All you have to do is pinch the folds of a Highway seam together and then bar-tack them.

## Aligned Intersections

A bulky seam should not join with another bulky seam, so it's necessary to use connectors, or sashings, to assemble Cotton Theory projects. It's also necessary to line up the seams on either side of the connectors, even though these seams do not actually intersect. This is called aligning the intersections.

This technique gives projects a professionally finished look.

### Follow these steps:

❖ Sew, fold, and finish one side of the connector.

❖ Place a ruler along an intersecting finished seam, as shown in the illustration.

❖ Place a pin in the raw edge of the connector to mark the spot that lines up with the seam.

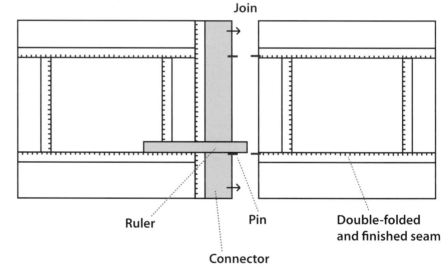

Join

Ruler    Pin    Double-folded and finished seam

Connector

❖ Align the pin with the corresponding finished seam on the quilt section you are connecting.

❖ Follow the above steps for other seams.

❖ Match up the pins and seams, and sew the connector to the quilt section.

## Quilted Embroidery

Machine embroidery designs can be used to quilt pieces of Cotton Theory projects. You simply place all three layers — back-side fabric, batting and front-side fabric — in a machine embroidery hoop and embroider as usual. Select good-quality thread, and choose thread colors for the back side as well as the front side of the embroidery, because the finished project will be reversible.

Look for embroidery designs that are outlines or are not very full (less dense). Avoid wide satin-stitch outlines because it is difficult to lock the tension in the middle on these. You may be able to disguise imperfect tension with thread choices. Variegated threads are great to use on top of your machine and in the bobbin. It's a good idea to do a practice piece first when embroidering.

It may be necessary to increase the upper tension on the sewing machine. Rayon 40-weight threads, commonly used for embroidery, need a looser upper tension of 2.0 to 2.5 mm (metric scale). Cotton 40-weight and 50-weight threads, used in Cotton Theory projects, usually need a tighter upper tension of 3.0 to 3.5 mm.

Embroidery was used to quilt this block.

Add the fabric and batting layers to your machine hoop in one of two ways:

❖ If layers are large enough to stay in the hoop tightly, you do not need to use a layer of water-soluble stabilizer, because the batting will act as a stabilizer. Cutting fabric and batting pieces larger when you plan to add quilted embroidery may be helpful. However, you will need to trim the fabric and batting to the correct size later.

❖ If pieces are too small for the hoop, put a layer of water-soluble stabilizer in the hoop, and place your layered pieces on top of the stabilizer. Baste the layers to the stabilizer; then embroider the design. Remove basting and wash away the stabilizer after embroidering.

## Bobbin Work

You can feature bobbin work on the front side of projects by placing layers upside down on your sewing machine (back side fabric facing up). Thread choices and bobbin tension are important. Here's some advice:

Bobbin work adds an unusual decorative touch to projects.

❖ Heavy threads that are too large to fit through the eye of a machine needle can be wound on a bobbin and used for all aspects of Cotton Theory projects, from straight-line quilting to decorative quilting to topstitching to embroidery.

❖ Because it's almost impossible to lock the sewing machine's tension in the middle of the quilt layers, the top thread usually will appear on the back side of the layers as tiny dots. Therefore, top and bobbin threads should be the same color or should blend together when doing bobbin work so your finished bobbin embroidery is sharp and clear.

❖ Wind bobbins about three-fourths full. You can wind bobbins by machine if you bypass the thread guides. To determine how much thread is on the bobbin, first wind the bobbin; then take the thread off the bobbin, measure the yardage, and wind it back on the bobbin. After embroidering a design, measure the amount remaining on the bobbin.

❖ On many sewing machines, adjusting the bobbin tension requires a small, flat-head screwdriver. Turning the screw to the left loosens the tension. Adjust the screw in very small increments and test how the bobbin thread performs. It's a good idea to keep track of how much you loosen the tension.

❖ When working with heavy threads, begin and end with tiny stitches (straight stitch 0.5 mm long). Avoid 0.0 mm, because you will be stitching in place, and this will look like a knot.

# Stitches

Stitch suggestions are included in project chapters in this book. Measurements are given in metric scale, such as 3.5 mm.

## Quilting Stitches

You can quilt layered pieces with any stitches you have in your sewing machine. The batting acts as a stabilizer while quilting.

It's best to select quilting stitches that are light and not too dense. The tighter the stitch, the more the quilted pieces will tighten and draw up. Bobbin tension may need to be adjusted if you choose dense and tight decorative stitches along with heavier threads.

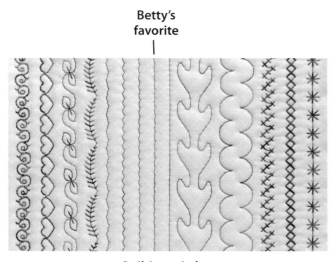

**Betty's favorite**

Quilting stitches

The photo above shows some stitch suggestions for quilting. You can adjust the width and length of stitches to suit your preferences and your project.

One superb quilting stitch is the wobble, which is 0.5 mm wide and 3.0 mm long. (It is marked "Betty's favorite" in the photo above.) This is a zigzag stitch altered so it looks like hand quilting, a little wobbly. It's a good stitch to choose, because no matter

how hard you try to quilt perfectly straight, you're going to wobble a bit. So, if you start out wobbling, this will make you perfect!

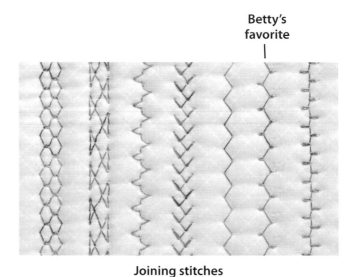

**Betty's favorite**

Joining stitches

## Joining Stitches

Joining stitches are used to topstitch the folds of Cotton Theory seams, as described in procedures listed in the Techniques chapter.

It is important that these stitches are light and airy so your quilt remains soft and easy to drape.

The photo above displays stitch possibilities. When topstitching, you may need to lengthen and widen stitches in your sewing machine to meet the needs of your project.

A stitch that works very well is the one marked "Betty's favorite" in the photo above. This joining stitch, which has been altered from the sewing machine's default, is 6.0 mm wide and 4.0 mm long. It is very forgiving and tends to hide less-than-perfect topstitching, because it has no middle point and only stitches in a forward motion.

## Directional Stitches

You can use directional stitches to topstitch the folds for the One-Way Street procedure, described in the Techniques chapter. However, it is important you stitch left to right, as shown in the adjacent photo. This way, the bulk of the quilt will go to the left of the sewing machine and will not build up in the throat area.

It will take practice to use directional stitches, because when you stitch in the ditch (on an existing seam), your needle needs to be positioned exactly on the seam line, or the stitching will be obvious on the back side of your project.

If your sewing machine has a mirror-image feature for stitches, be sure the direction is

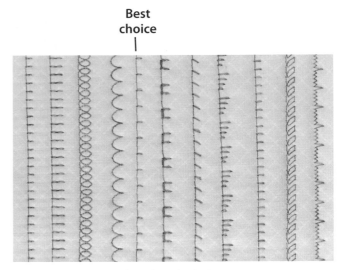

Best choice

Directional stitches

set to the right, as shown in the photo. If your directional stitches do not extend to the right, please do not use them for Cotton Theory projects.

# Skill Levels

Wondering which Cotton Theory project to sew first? Skill level designations on the first page of each project may help you decide. Projects range from Skill Level 1 to Skill Level 4.

Are you a beginning Cotton Theory quilter? Look for Skill Level 1. All you need are basic sewing and pressing skills, as well as basic cutting skills using a mat, ruler, and rotary cutter.

Are you already familiar with Cotton Theory quilting? Consider Skill Level 2 or Skill Level 3 projects.

Are you ready for a Cotton Theory challenge? Choose Skill Level 4.

- ❖ **Skill Level 1** = Beginner
- ❖ **Skill Level 2** = Advanced beginner
- ❖ **Skill Level 3** = Intermediate Cotton Theory quilter
- ❖ **Skill Level 4** = Advanced Cotton Theory quilter

# Part Three
# Cotton Theory Projects

This Feathered Fling Quilt features 49 hand-embroidered state birds.
The 50th state bird adorns a matching pillow. The quilt and pillow are
two of the 14 step-by-step projects in this book.

# Minuet Candle Mat

(10" x 10")

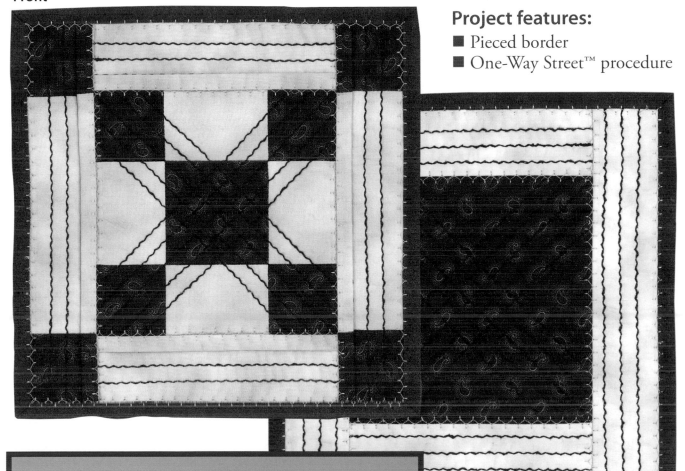

## Project features:
- Pieced border
- One-Way Street™ procedure

Back

## Basic block:
6" x 6" Nine-Patch Block
(8" x 8" unfinished)

**Dress up a table or shelf
with this reversible Minuet Candle Mat.**

## Yardage Requirements

*Based on 42-inch wide fabric*

### Front Side and Back Side

*Two fat quarters will provide enough fabric to construct both sides.*

1 fat quarter burgundy print

1 fat quarter beige

### Binding

⅛ yd. dark green

### Batting

Cotton Theory Batting, 18" x 10", or scraps that you have available

## Fabric Cutting Instructions

Cut carefully to ensure you have an adequate amount of fabric. Label your cut pieces for each side of the project.

### Beige fat quarter

**Front Side**
  **A:** Cut 4– 3" x 3"
  **C:** Cut 2– 3" x 8"
  **D:** Cut 2– 3" x 6½"

**Back Side**
  **C:** Cut 2– 3" x 8"
  **D:** Cut 2– 3" x 10"

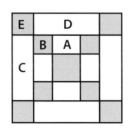

**Front side of candle mat**

### Burgundy fat quarter

**Front Side**
  **B:** Cut 5– 3" x 3"
  **E:** Cut 4– 3" x 2¼"

**Back Side**
  **Back of block:** Cut 1– 8" x 8"

### Binding

Cut 1– 2½" x 42" strip

## Batting Cutting Instructions

**Block:** Cut 1– 6" x 6"
**C:** Cut 2– 2" x 6"
**D:** Cut 2– 2" x 10"

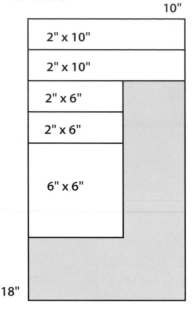

**Cutting diagram
for Cotton Theory Batting (18" x 10")**
*(Gray area denotes batting that is not used)*

## Piecing Instructions

Insert universal needle size 80/12 into sewing machine.

### Nine-Patch Block

1.  With right sides together and using a ¼" seam, sew squares A and B together, as shown in diagram.

2.  Press seams open.

3.  Sew the three sections together.

4.  Press seams open.

### Front-Side Borders

1.  With right sides together and using a ¼" seam, sew E to both ends of D, as shown in diagram.

2.  Press seams open.

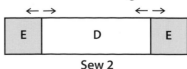

**Sew 2**

32

# Quilting Instructions

Insert quilting needle size 90/14 into sewing machine. For best results, use a walking foot when quilting layers.

**Thread suggestion:** 50-weight dark red cotton on top and in bobbin.

**Stitch suggestion:** Zigzag stitch 0.5 mm wide and 3.0 mm long (wobble stitch).

## Nine-Patch Block

1. Layer fabric and batting. With back of block (burgundy 8" x 8") right side down, place batting in center, and place Nine-Patch Block right side up.

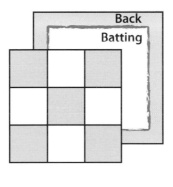

2. Press layers together with steam.

3. Mark an X across Nine-Patch Block.

4. Quilt on the X with a wobble stitch, quilting through all layers.

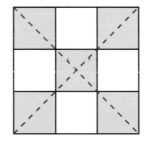

5. Using edge of presser foot as a guide, quilt two more rows on each side of the X, as shown in diagram (total of five rows in each diagonal direction).

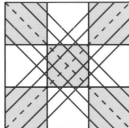

## Borders

1. Layer fabric and batting, placing back-side rectangle C (beige 3" x 8") right side down,

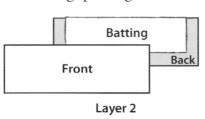

Layer 2

batting even with one long side of rectangle (as shown in diagram), and front-side C (beige 3" x 8") right side up.

2. Press layers together with steam.

3. Layer back-side rectangle D (beige 3" x 10") right side down, placing batting even with one long side of rectangle (as shown in previous diagram), and front-side D/E rectangle (burgundy and beige) right side up. (Layer two.)

4. Press layers together with steam.

5. Place Cotton Theory Adhesive Quilting Guide 1⅜" to the right of sewing machine needle.

*Betty's Advice: Use the Cotton Theory Adhesive Quilting Guide to produce straight quilting rows and accurate seam allowances.*

6. Quilt 1⅜" from long side that has no batting in the seam allowance. (Quilt through entire length of rectangles.)

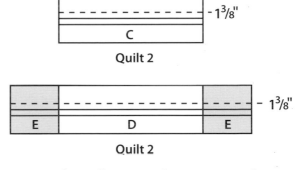

Quilt 2

Quilt 2

7. Using edge of presser foot as a guide, quilt two more rows toward other long side of rectangle, as shown in diagrams (total of three rows).

## Assembly Instructions

Insert topstitch needle size 90/14 into sewing machine.

Seam allowances will be 1" and will be finished on front side of project using the One-Way Street procedure, described in Techniques chapter.

**Thread suggestion:** 50-weight beige cotton on top and in bobbin.

**Stitch suggestion:** Straight stitch 3.5 mm long; joining stitch 6.0 mm wide and 4.0 mm long.

1. With back sides together (back fabrics against each other), sew border C (long edge without batting) to sides of Nine-Patch Block. Use a 1" seam, and stitch through all layers.

2. Press the back side; then press all seam allowances on front side toward border C.

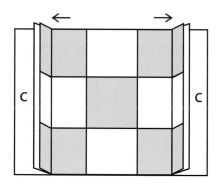

3. Fold and finish seam allowances using the One-Way Street procedure, explained in Techniques chapter.

4. With back sides together and using a 1" seam, sew border D/E (long edge without batting) to top and bottom of Nine-Patch Block. (Be sure to align seams, as described in Techniques chapter.)

5. Press the back side; then press all seam allowances on front side toward border D/E.

6. Finish seams using the One-Way Street procedure.

## Binding

Because batting on this project goes all the way to the raw edges, there is no need to trim fabric before applying binding.

For instructions, see Binding chapter near end of this book, but do not trim fabric.

# Nine-Patch Polka Quilt

(87" x 87")

**Project features:**

- Back-to-back blocks
- Pieced borders and sashings
- Block shrinkage due to 1" seam allowances
- Highway™ procedure
- One-Way Street™ procedure
- Merging Lancs™ procedure on connectors

Stunning stars stand out on a field of light-colored fabric in this Nine-Patch Polka Quilt. Pieced borders and sashings create the stars on the front side of this reversible quilt. A vivid mixture of colors brings a completely different look to the back side, shown on the next page.

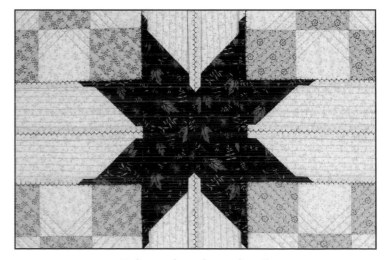

**Enlarged to show detail**

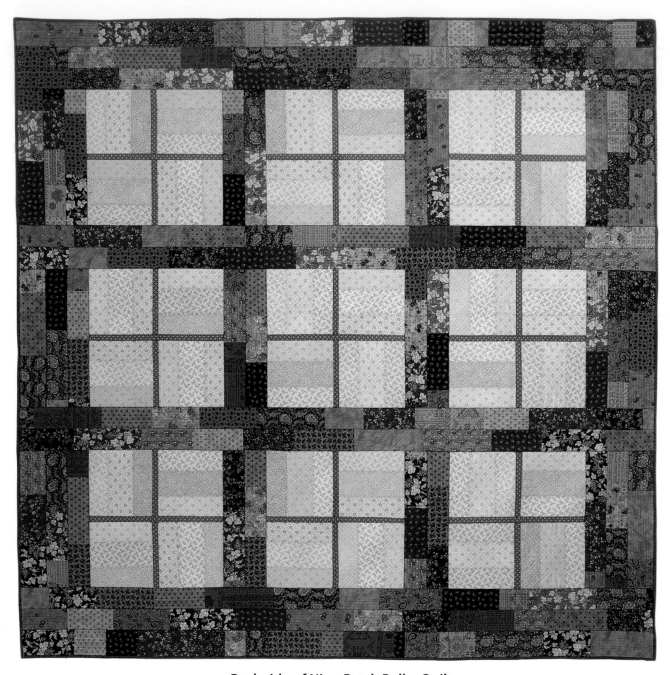

**Back side of Nine-Patch Polka Quilt**

## Basic blocks:

36– 9" x 9" Nine-Patch Blocks
for front side (11" x 11" unfinished)

36– 9" x 9" Fence Rail Blocks for back
side (11" x 11" unfinished)

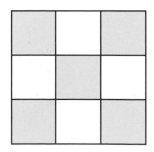

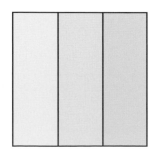

## Yardage Requirements

*Based on 42-inch wide fabric*

*See finished diagrams at end of this chapter for placement of pieces.*

### Front Side

**Nine-Patch Blocks:**
1½ yd. cream and
⅝ yd. each of 3 assorted light prints

**Block Connectors A and B:**
⅝ yd. green and
⅝ yd. brown

**Short Sashing D, Long Sashings C and E, Square H, and Borders I and J:** 5¾ yd. cream

*(The letter F is not used for identification in this quilt.)*

**Star Points G and K:**
6 assorted green fat quarters and
6 assorted brown fat quarters

### Back Side

**Fence Rail Blocks:** 1½ yd. each of 3 assorted light prints

**Block Connectors A and B:** 1¼ yd. green

**Short Sashing D, Long Sashings, and Borders G/H, I, J:** 22 assorted fat quarters in green, brown, red, blue, and gold.

*Leftover yardage from sashing stars on front side will be equivalent to three fat quarters. If you use this on back side, you only will need 19 fat quarters, instead of 22.*

### Binding

⅝ yd. brown

### Batting

Cotton Theory Batting, 18" x 13 yd.

## Fabric Cutting Instructions

Cut carefully to ensure you have an adequate amount of fabric. Label your cut pieces for each side of the project.

Where strips are listed, cut them on the crosswise grain (selvage to selvage); then cut sub-cuts from each strip on the lengthwise grain. (See diagrams in Preparation chapter for details.)

### Front Side

**Nine-Patch Blocks:**

> **From cream fabric:**
> Cut 12– 4" x 42" strips
>
> **From each of 3 assorted light prints:**
> Cut 5– 4" x 42" strips (total of 15 strips)

**Block Connectors A and B:**

> **From green:**
> Cut 1– 20¾" strip
> **B:** Sub-cut 5– 2¾" x 20¾"
> **A:** Sub-cut 10– 2¾" x 11"
>
> **From brown:**
> Cut 1– 20¾" strip
> **B:** Sub-cut 4– 2¾" x 20¾"
> **A:** Sub-cut 8– 2¾" x 11"

**Short Sashing D (cream):**
Cut 4– 20¾" strips
Sub-cut 30– 5" x 20¾"

**Long Sashing C (cream):**
Cut 2– 20¾" strips
Sub-cut 16– 5" x 20¾"

**Long Sashing E (cream):**
Cut 1– 29¾" strip
Sub-cut 8– 5" x 29¾"

*More cutting instructions on next page*

## Square H (cream):
Cut 2– 5" strips
Sub-cut 16– 5" x 5"

## Borders I and J (cream):
Cut 1– 29¾" strip
**I:** Sub-cut 4– 5" x 29¾"
**J:** Sub-cut 2– 5" x 20¾

## Star Points G and K:
**From each of 6 assorted green fat quarters and 6 assorted brown fat quarters:**
**K:** Cut 2– 5" x 14"
**G:** Cut 4– 5" x 5"
*See fabric cutting diagram at bottom of this column.*

**Please label the assorted greens and browns with the letters K and G and also with the following color code:**
BR1 = Brown 1
GR1 = Green 1
BR2 = Brown 2
GR2 = Green 2
BR3 = Brown 3
GR3 = Green 3
BR4 = Brown 4
GR4 = Green 4
BR5 = Brown 5
GR5 = Green 5
BR6 = Brown 6
GR6 = Green 6

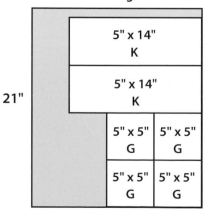

**Selvage**

**21"**

**18"**

**Fabric cutting diagram for Star Points G and K**
*(Gray area denotes fabric that is not used)*

## Back Side

### Fence Rail Blocks:
**From each of 3 assorted light prints:**
Cut 12– 4" x 42" strips
(total of 36 strips)

### Block Connectors A and B (green):
**A:** Cut 2– 11" strips
Sub-cut 18– 2¾" x 11"
**B:** Cut 1– 20¾" strip
Sub-cut 9– 2¾" x 20¾"

### Sashings and Borders:
*The sashings and borders of this quilt are meant to be scrappy.*
**From each of 22 assorted fat quarters:**
Cut 4– 5" x 18" (total of 88)
Sub-cut 8 in various lengths, such as 5" x 10" and 5" x 8", and 5" x 12" and 5" x 6" (total of 176)
*See fabric cutting diagrams below.*

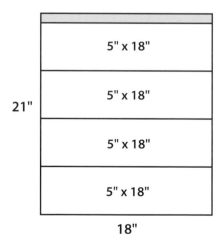

**Fabric cutting diagrams
for back-side Sashings and Borders**
*(Gray area denotes fabric that is not used)*

*More cutting instructions on next page*

With right sides together and using a ¼" seam, piece together the 5" edges of various colors and lengths of Sashing/Border segments randomly. Press seams open.

**Cut the following pieces:**
*Please label your cut pieces.*
**Long Sashings:** Cut 8– 5" x 88¼"
**Short Sashing D:** Cut 30– 5" x 20¾"
**Border I:** Cut 4– 5" x 29¾"
**Border J:** Cut 2– 5" x 20¾"
**Squares G/H:** Cut 16– 5" x 5"

## Binding

Cut 8– 2½" x 42" strips

## Batting Cutting Instructions

Cut longest pieces of batting first. Please label your cut pieces.

*See cutting diagrams on this page and the next page.*

**Blocks:** Cut 36– 9" x 9"

**Block Connector A:** Cut 18– ¾" x 9"

**Block Connector B:** Cut 9– ¾" x 18¾"

**Long Sashings:** Cut 8– 3" x 88¼"

**Short Sashing D With Star Points:**
Cut 24– 3" x 18¾"

**Short Sashing D Without Star Points:**
Cut 6– 4" x 18¾"

**Border I:** Cut 4– 4" x 28¾"

**Border J:** Cut 2– 4" x 18¾"

**Squares G/H:** Cut 8– 3" x 4"

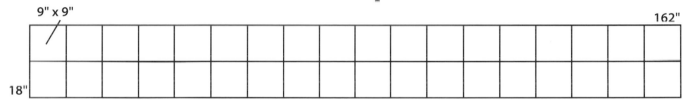

Cutting diagrams for Cotton Theory Batting (18" x 162", 18" x 88¼", and 18" x 113¾")
*(Gray area denotes batting that is not used)*

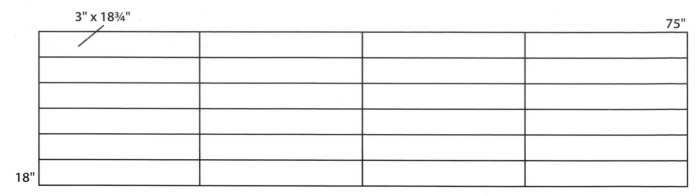

3" x 18¾"

75"

18"

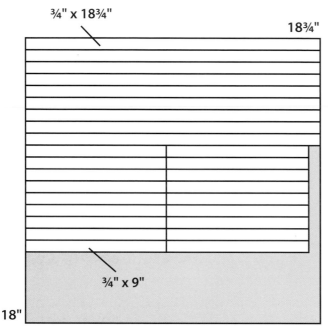

¾" x 18¾"

18¾"

¾" x 9"

18"

**Cutting diagrams for Cotton Theory Batting
(18" x 75" and 18" x 18¾")**

*(Gray area denotes batting that is not used)*

## Piecing Instructions

Insert universal needle size 80/12 into sewing machine.

Please label Rows 1 through 8 after piecing.

### Row 1 of Front-Side Long Sashing

1. Mark a 45-degree diagonal line on wrong side of Star Point K rectangle (Brown 1).

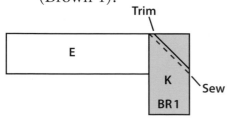

Trim

E

K

BR 1

Sew

**Note:** It is important to mark and sew diagonal lines accurately.

2. With right sides together, sew K (Brown 1) to Long Sashing E on diagonal line, as shown in diagram at bottom of previous column.

3. Trim seam to ¼".

4. Press seam open.

5. Mark a 45-degree diagonal line on wrong side of Long Sashing C.

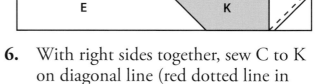

E          K          C

6. With right sides together, sew C to K on diagonal line (red dotted line in diagram).

7. Trim seam to ¼", and press seam open.

8. Sew K (Green 1) to C in same manner.

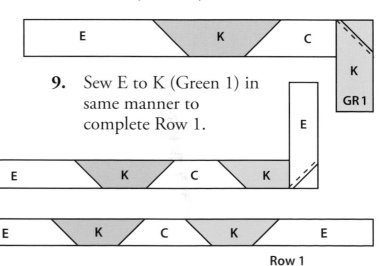

9. Sew E to K (Green 1) in same manner to complete Row 1.

Row 1

## Row 2 of Front-Side Long Sashing

*The piecing in Row 2 is a mirror image of Row 1.*

1.  Mark a 45-degree diagonal line on wrong side of K (Brown 1).

    **Note:** It is important to use the same color K as in Row 1. The pieces will form a star when fully assembled.

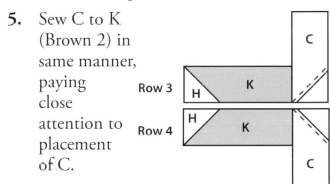

2.  With right sides together, sew K (Brown 1) to E on diagonal line (red dotted line in diagram above).

3.  Trim seam to ¼" (black diagonal line in diagram above).

4.  Press seam open.

5.  Sew C to K (Brown 1) in same manner.

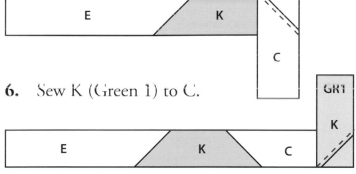

6.  Sew K (Green 1) to C.

7.  Sew E to K (Green 1) to complete Row 2.

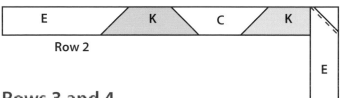

## Rows 3 and 4 of Front-Side Long Sashing

*Rows 3 and 4 are mirror images of each other.*

1.  Mark a 45-degree diagonal line on wrong side of Square H.

2.  With right sides together, sew Square H to Star Point K (Brown 2) on diagonal line (red dotted line), paying close attention to placement of Square H for Rows 3 and 4.

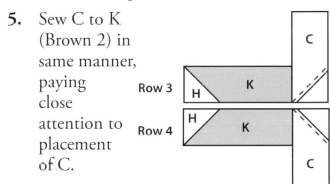

3.  Trim seam to ¼".

4.  Press seam open.

5.  Sew C to K (Brown 2) in same manner, paying close attention to placement of C.

6.  Sew K (Green 2) to C in same manner.

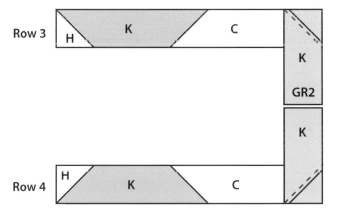

7.  Sew C to K (Green 2).

**8.** Sew K (Brown 3) to C.

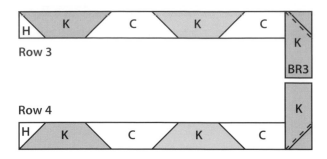

**9.** Sew C to K (Brown 3).

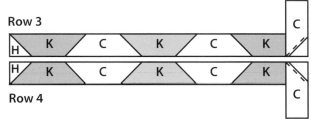

**10.** Sew K (Green 3) to C.

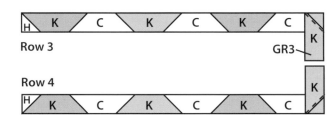

**11.** Sew Square H to K (Green 3) to complete Rows 3 and 4.

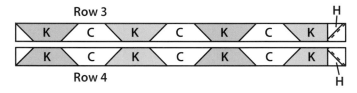

## Rows 5 and 6 of Front-Side Long Sashing

**1.** Construct in same manner as Rows 3 and 4, using K (Green 4), K (Brown 4), K (Green 5) and K (Brown 5). Remember to label your rows.

## Rows 7 and 8 of Front-Side Long Sashing

**1.** Construct in same manner as Rows 1 and 2, using K (Green 6) and K (Brown 6).

## Front-Side Short Sashing

**1.** Mark a diagonal line on wrong side of 40 Star Point G squares. (Half of the squares should be mirror images of the others.)

**2.** With right sides together, place G squares on Short Sashing D in positions shown in diagrams. Pay close attention to color of G squares.

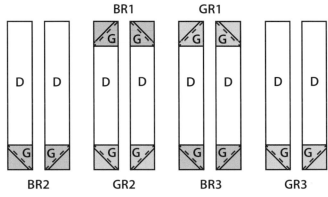

Short Sashings between Row 2 and Row 3

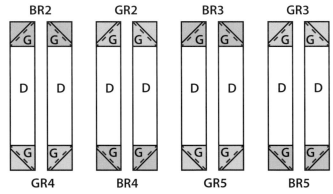

Short Sashings between Row 4 and Row 5

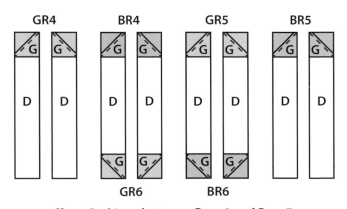

Short Sashings between Row 6 and Row 7

3. Sew G to D on diagonal lines (red dotted lines in diagrams on previous page).

4. Trim seams to ¼" (black diagonal lines in diagrams on previous page).

5. Press seams open.

**Note:** Please label Short Sashings for the appropriate rows. There will be six additional Short Sashings D without any Star Points.

## Remaining Front-Side Star Points

1. With right sides together, place remaining eight H squares on remaining eight Star Point G squares so that H covers G.

2. Mark a diagonal line on the wrong side of H.

3. Sew on diagonal line, as shown in diagram.

4. Trim ¼" from seam line.

5. Press seam open.

6. Set G/H squares aside.

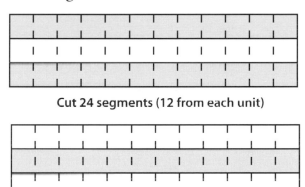

Sew 8

## Nine-Patch Blocks

1. Arrange four cream strips (4"x 42") and five matching light print strips (4"x 42") as shown in diagrams below and in next column.

2. With right sides together and using a ¼" seam, sew together the long sides of one light print, one cream, and another of same light print.

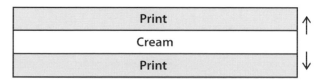

Sew 2 with the same fabrics

3. Press seams toward print strips.

4. Repeat Steps 2 and 3 so you have two units with the same light print.

5. With right sides together and using a ¼" seam, sew together one cream strip, one light print strip (same print as Step 2), and another cream strip.

| Cream |
| Print |
| Cream |

Sew 1

6. Press seams toward print strip.

7. Cut units into 3½" segments, as shown in diagrams below.

Cut 24 segments (12 from each unit)

Cut 12 segments

8. Arrange segments as shown in diagram.

9. With right sides together and using a ¼" seam, sew segments together into Nine-Patch Blocks.

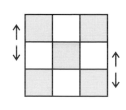

Sew 12

10. Press seams open.

11. Repeat Steps 1 through 10 for remaining cream and light print strips.

12. You will have a total of 36 Nine-Patch Blocks.

## Fence Rail Blocks

1. With right sides together and using a ¼" seam, sew together the long sides of three assorted light print strips, as shown in diagram.

Sew 12

2. Press seams open.

3. Repeat Steps 1 and 2 to make a total of 12 pieced units.

4. Cut each unit into 11" segments, as shown in diagram, to create a total of 36 Fence Rail Blocks.

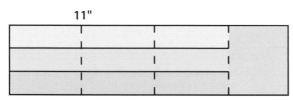

11"

**Cut 3– 11" segments from each of 12 units
(total of 36 segments)**
*(Gray area denotes fabric that is not used)*

# Quilting Instructions

Insert quilting needle size 90/14 into sewing machine. For best results, use a walking foot when quilting layers.

**Thread suggestion:** 50-weight cotton in top and bobbin. Match thread to fabrics for each side.

**Stitch suggestion:** Zigzag 0.5 mm wide and 3.0 mm long (wobble stitch).

## Nine-Patch and Fence Rail Blocks

1. Layer fabric and batting. Place Fence Rail Block right side down, batting in center, and Nine-Patch Block right side up.

**Note:** Seams of Fence Rail Block should be vertical.

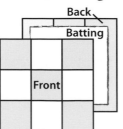

2. Press layers together with steam.

3. Mark an X across Nine-Patch Block.

4. Quilt on the X using wobble stitch.

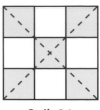

Quilt 36

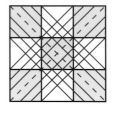

5. Using edge of presser foot as a guide, quilt three more rows on each side of the X, as shown in diagram (total of seven rows in each direction).

## Block Connectors A and B

1. Layer back fabric right side down, batting in center, and front fabric right side up.

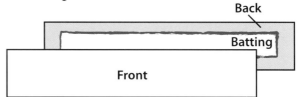

2. Press layers together with steam.

3. Place Adhesive Quilting Guide 1⅜" to right of sewing machine needle to provide a straight quilting row.

4. Using a wobble stitch, quilt down the middle of Block Connectors A and B. (Quilt through entire length of connectors.)

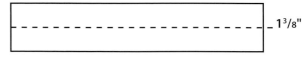

1³⁄₈"

**Quilt 18 of Block Connector A
Quilt 9 of Block Connector B**

## Short Sashing D With Star Points

1. Layer back fabric right side down, batting in center, and front fabric right side up.

2. Press layers together with steam.

**Note:** Because the Cotton Theory 1" seam allowances will be folded and topstitched on the outside of the project, there should be no quilting within ¾" of the raw edges on the long sides of Short Sashing D.

3. Starting in corner and using a wobble stitch, quilt in the ditch on Star Point 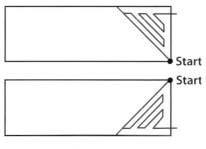 seam line, and pivot ¾" from raw edge. Then sew about five stitches, pivot, and quilt one presser-foot width away from previous quilting. Quilt a total of four rows in this manner, as shown in diagram.

4. Place Adhesive Quilting Guide 2½" to right of sewing machine needle.

5. Quilt down the middle of Short Sashing D, pivoting at Star Point seam line, sewing about five stitches in the ditch, pivoting again, and then quilting one presser-foot width away from previous quilting.

6. Quilt a total of three rows on both sides of middle in this manner for all Short Sashings With Star Points. End with backstitch. (Quilt channels should measure about ⅜".)

7. Short Sashings that have Star Points on both ends should be layered and quilted in same manner. See Steps 1 through 6.

## Short Sashing D Without Star Points

1. With back fabric right side down, layer batting even with one long edge of sashing, and place front fabric right side up.

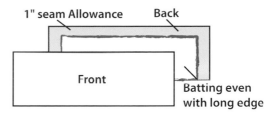

2. Press layers together with steam.

3. Place Adhesive Quilting Guide 2½" to right of sewing machine needle.

4. Quilt down the middle of sashing.

5. Using edge of presser foot as a guide, quilt three rows away from middle on the side that has no batting in seam allowance, and quilt five rows on the side that has batting to the edge. Alternate directions while quilting to compensate for fabric shifting.

## Rows 1 through 8 of Long Sashing

1. Layer back fabric, batting, and front fabric, and press layers together with steam.

**Note:** Batting will be even with raw edges on short sides of sashing.

2. Secure layers with pins.

3. Quilt in same manner as Short Sashing D With Star Points. Stitch six (instead of four) short, diagonal rows in the Star Point K areas, as shown in diagram below, and quilt horizontal rows in the E and C areas.

Row 1 of Long Sashing                    Quilt Rows 1 through 8

## Border J

1. With back fabric right side down, layer batting even with one long edge of Border J, and place front fabric right side up.

2. Press layers together with steam.

3. Place Adhesive Quilting Guide 2½" to right of sewing machine needle.

4. Quilt down the middle of Border J.

5. Continue quilting in same manner as Short Sashing D Without Star Points. Using edge of presser foot as a guide, quilt three rows away from middle on the side that has no batting in seam allowance, and quilt five rows on the side that has batting to the edge. Alternate directions while quilting to compensate for fabric shifting.

## Border I

1. With back fabric right side down, layer batting even with two edges of Border I, as shown in diagrams, and place front fabric right side up.

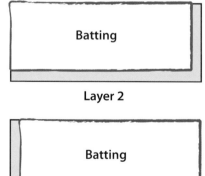

2. Press layers together with steam.

3. Quilt in same manner as Border J.

## Squares G/H

1. With back-side G/H square right side down, layer batting even with top edge of back square, and place front G/H square right side up, as shown in diagram.

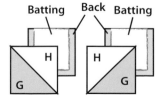

2. Press layers together with steam.

3. Quilt in the ditch of diagonal seam.

4. Quilt four additional rows on each side of seam line, stopping ¾" from raw edges and pivoting where needed.

## Assembly Instructions

Insert topstitch needle size 90/14 into sewing machine.

Seam allowances will be finished on front side of this project using the One-Way Street™ and Highway™ procedures, described in Techniques chapter.

**Note:** Use a 1" seam allowance when sewing your quilted pieces together.

**Thread suggestion:** 40-weight dark variegated cotton on top and 50-weight dark brown cotton in bobbin.

**Stitch suggestion:** Straight stitch 3.5 mm long; joining stitch 6.0 mm wide and 4.0 mm long.

*Betty's Advice:*
*Use the Cotton Theory Adhesive Quilting Guide for accurate 1" seam allowances.*

## Nine-Patch Blocks

*Four Nine-Patch Blocks will be assembled into one large block using Block Connectors.*

1. Arrange Nine-Patch Blocks to your liking in groups of four, and alternate the direction of Fence Rail Blocks on the back side. (Refer to quilt diagrams at end of chapter for placement of blocks.)

**2.** With back sides together (back fabrics against each other) and using a 1" seam, sew Block Connector A to right-hand side of Nine-Patch Block, as shown in diagram. Sew through all layers.

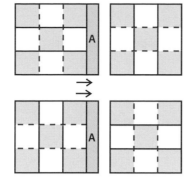

**Construct 9 groups**
**(5 with green connectors and 4 with brown connectors)**
*(Red lines indicate direction of Fence Rail Blocks on back side.)*

**3.** Press the back side; then press all seam allowances on front side toward Block Connector A.

**4.** Finish seams using the One-Way Street procedure, explained in Techniques chapter.

**5.** With back sides together, sew Nine-Patch Block to other side of Block Connector A.

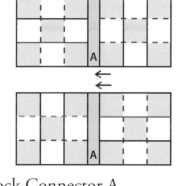

**6.** Press seam allowances on front toward Block Connector A.

**7.** Finish seams using the One-Way Street procedure.

**Note:** Block Connector A finishes at ¾". When you fold and topstitch the seam allowances, the actual connector will be hidden beneath the folds. This is called Merging Lanes.

**8.** With back sides together, sew matching green or brown Block Connector B to bottom of upper Nine-Patch unit.

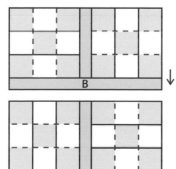

**9.** Press seam allowances on front side toward Block Connector B.

**10.** Finish seam using the One-Way Street procedure.

**11.** With back sides together, sew lower Nine-Patch unit to upper unit. Remember to align intersections, as described in Techniques chapter.

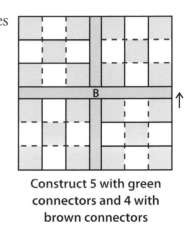

**Construct 5 with green connectors and 4 with brown connectors**

**12.** Press seam allowances on front side toward Block Connector B.

**13.** Finish seam using the One-Way Street procedure.

**14.** Arrange Nine-Patch units in order shown in finished quilt diagram at end of this chapter.

## Short Sashing D

*When the Short Sashings and Long Sashings are sewn into place, they will form a star at their intersections.*

**1.** Arrange Short Sashing D pieces so that Star Point colors are in their appropriate places. (Refer to Short Sashing piecing instructions and the finished quilt diagram at end of this chapter for placement of Short Sashings.)

**2.** With back sides together and using a 1" seam, sew appropriate Short Sashing D to left and right-hand sides of all Nine-Patch units, as indicated in diagram on next page.

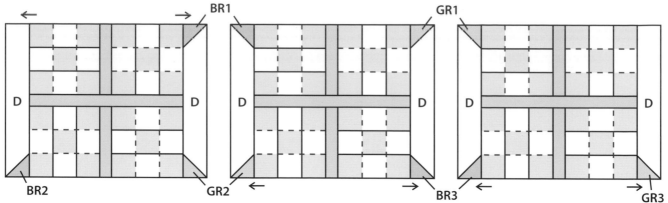

**These Nine-Patch units are between Sashing Rows 2 and 3, as indicated on finished quilt diagram at end of chapter**
*(Star Point positions for other Nine-Patch units will vary)*

**3.** Press seam allowances on front side toward Short Sashing D.

**4.** Finish seams using the One-Way Street procedure.

**5.** With back sides together, connect the Nine-Patch units.

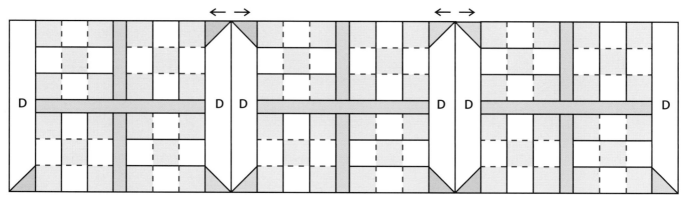

**Construct 3** *(Star Point positions for other Nine-Patch units will vary)*

**6.** Press seams open.

**7.** Finish seams using the Highway procedure, described in Techniques chapter.

**8.** With back sides together, sew appropriate Short Sashings D to sides of each Nine-Patch row, as shown in diagram below. Pay close attention to batting placement on Sashing D Without Star Points. The seam allowances do not have batting.

**9.** Press seams open, and finish seams using the Highway procedure.

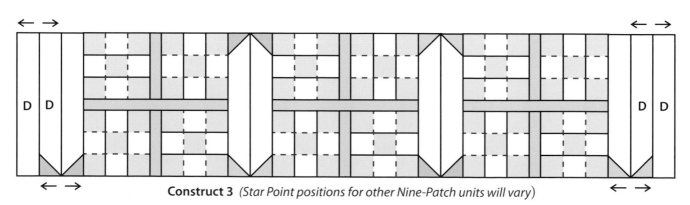

**Construct 3** *(Star Point positions for other Nine-Patch units will vary)*

## Rows 1 through 8 of Long Sashings

1. With back sides together, sew Row 1 of Long Sashing to Row 2.

Row 1

Row 2  *(Star Point positions in other Long Sashing rows will vary)*

2. Press seam open.

3. Finish seam using the Highway procedure.

4. Repeat Steps 1 through 3 for Rows 3 and 4, Rows 5 and 6, and Rows 7 and 8.

## Attaching Long Sashings

1. Refer to finished quilt diagram for placement of Long Sashing rows.

2. With back sides together, sew appropriate Long Sashing rows to top, bottom, and between Nine-Patch rows. Remember to align intersections as needed.

3. Press seam allowances toward Long Sashing.

4. Finish seams using the One-Way Street procedure.

## Top and Bottom Border Rows

1. Refer to finished quilt diagram for placement of border pieces I, J, and G/H.

2. With back sides together, sew two G/H Star Point squares together, paying close attention to color of G and to placement of batting. The seam allowances do not have batting.

3. Press seams open, and finish with the Highway procedure.

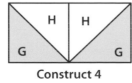

Construct 4

4. Sew remaining G/H Star Point squares in same manner.

5. Sew G/H Star Point units to Border I and Border J, paying close attention to position of pieces and color of G.

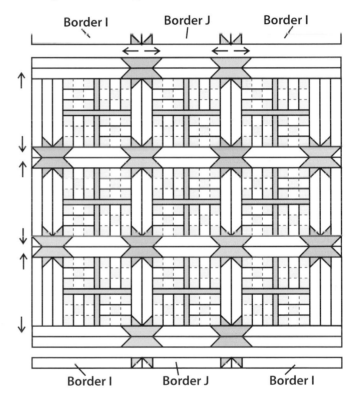

6. Press seam allowances toward G/H, and finish with One-Way Street procedure.

7. Attach top and bottom border rows to quilt.

8. Press seam allowances toward border rows, and finish with the One-Way Street procedure.

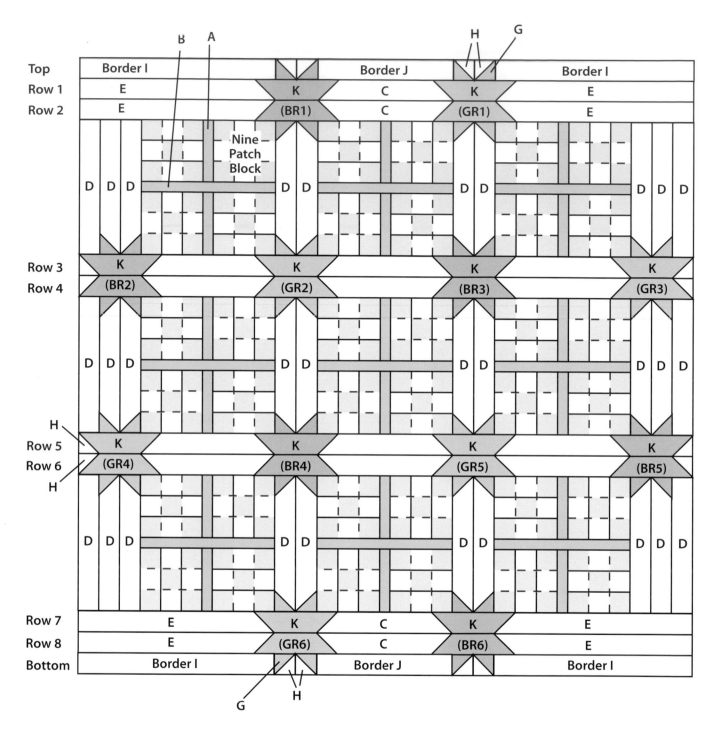

**Front side of finished Nine-Patch Polka Quilt**

*(Red lines indicate direction of Fence Rail Blocks on back side of quilt)*

# Binding

1. Because batting extends to the raw edges of this quilt, there is no need for trimming before binding is applied.

2. For instructions on applying binding, see Binding chapter near end of this book, but do not trim.

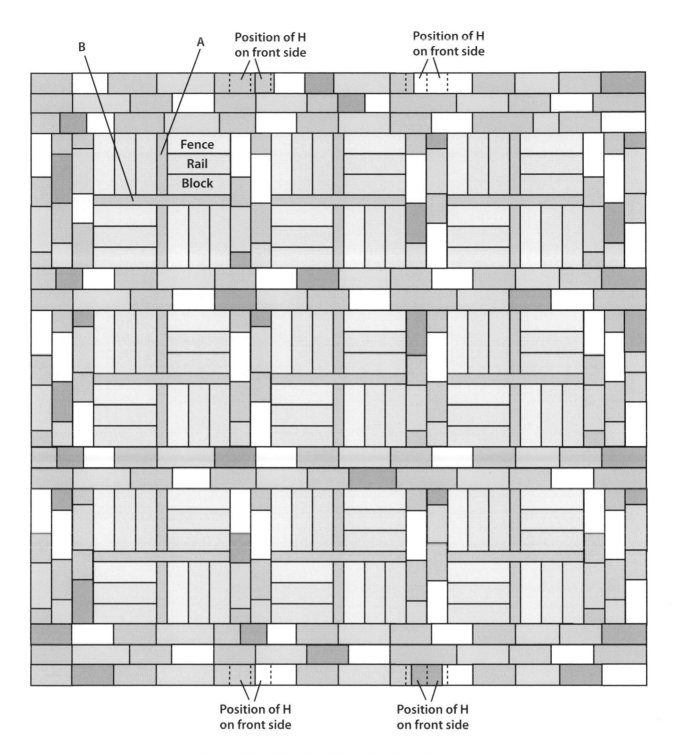

B A

Position of H on front side

Position of H on front side

Fence Rail Block

Position of H on front side

Position of H on front side

Back side of finished Nine-Patch Polka Quilt

# Feathered Fling Quilt

## (101" x 104")

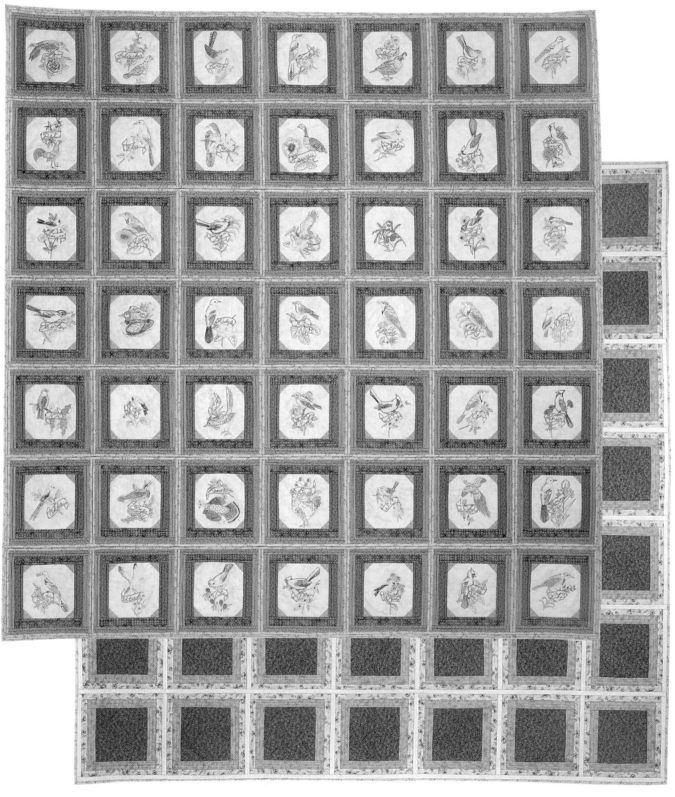

**Hand-embroidered birds adorn the front of this reversible, king-size Cotton Theory quilt. Turn the quilt over, and you'll see blocks in shades of coral pink and cream. Instructions begin on the next page.**

**Basic block:** 49– 8½" x 9" embroidered blocks (10½" x 11" unfinished)

**Project features:**

■ Hand-done embroidery
■ One-Way Street™ procedure
■ Merging Lanes™ procedure on connectors

*Blocks in this quilt were hand-embroidered using Aunt Martha's Hot Iron Transfers, Design 626, State Birds, All Fifty States. Forty-nine blocks were sewn into the quilt, and one was used to make a matching pillow. The hot iron transfers are available through the Quilt Yard, Osseo, Wisconsin; phone (715) 597-2452 or (800) 673-8075.*

## Yardage Requirements

*Based on 42-inch wide fabric*

*See quilt diagram at end of this chapter for placement of pieces.*

### Front Side

**Block for Embroidery:**
4¼ yd. cream

**Half-Square Triangles:**
1¾ yd. soft gold

**Rectangle 1:** 2⅞ yd. dark pink

**Rectangle 2:** 3½ yd. dark green

**Rectangle 3:** 3⅜ yd. medium pink

**Rectangle 4:** 3⅝ yd. medium green

**Short Connector 5:** 1⅞ yd. light pink

**Long Connector 6:** 1¾ yd. light green

### Back Side

**Back of Block:**
4¼ yd. dark pink print

**Rectangles 1 and 2:** Total of 6⅜ yd. medium pink

**Rectangles 3 and 4:** Total of 7 yd. cream/pink print

**Short Connector 5 and Long Connector 6:**
3⅝ yd. cream tone-on-tone

### Binding
⅞ yd. light green

### Batting
Cotton Theory Batting, 18" x 17½ yd.

## Fabric Cutting Instructions

Cut carefully to ensure you have an adequate amount of fabric. Label your cut pieces for each side of the project.

Where strips are listed, cut them on the crosswise grain (selvage to selvage); then cut sub-cuts from each strip on the lengthwise grain. (See diagrams in Preparation chapter for details.)

### Front Side

**Block for Embroidery (cream):**
Cut 13– 11" strips
Sub-cut 50– 10½" x 11"

**Half-Square Triangles (soft gold):**
Cut 17– 3½" strips
Sub-cut 200– 3½" x 3½"

**Rectangle 1 (dark pink):**
Cut 9– 11" strips
Sub-cut 100– 3½" x 11"

**Rectangle 2 (dark green):**
Cut 9– 13½" strips
Sub-cut 100– 3½" x 13½"

**Rectangle 3 (medium pink):**
Cut 8– 14" strips
Sub-cut 100– 3" x 14"

**Rectangle 4 (medium green):**
Cut 8– 15½" strips
Sub-cut 100– 3" x 15½"

**Short Connector 5 (light pink):**
Cut 4– 16" strips
Sub-cut 56– 2¾" x 16"

**Long Connector 6 (light green):**
Cut 1– 60" strip
Sub-cut 15– 2¾" x 60"

Piece together the 15 sub-cuts end-to-end
with a ¼" seam; press seams open.
Then cut 8 connectors– 2¾" x 102½"

## Back Side

### Back of Block (dark pink print):
Cut 13– 11" strips
Sub-cut 50– 10½" x 11"

### Rectangle 1 (medium pink):
Cut 9– 11" strips
Sub-cut 100– 3½" x 11"

**Rectangle 2 (medium pink):**
Cut 9– 13½" strips
Sub-cut 100– 3½" x 13½"

**Rectangle 3 (cream/pink print):**
Cut 8– 14" strips
Sub-cut 100– 3" x 14"

**Rectangle 4 (cream/pink print):**
Cut 8– 15½" strips
Sub-cut 100– 3" x 15½"

**Short Connector 5 (cream tone-on-tone):**
Cut 4– 16" strips
Sub-cut 56– 2¾" x 16"

**Long Connector 6 (cream tone-on-tone):**
Cut 1– 60" strip
Sub-cut 15– 2¾" x 60"

Piece together the 15 sub-cuts end-to-end
with a ¼" seam; press seams open.
Then cut 8 connectors– 2¾" x 102½"

## Binding

Cut 11– 2½" x 42" strips

## Batting Cutting Instructions

Cut longest pieces of batting first. Please
label your cut pieces.

**Embroidered Block:** Cut 50– 8½" x 9"

**Rectangle 1:** Cut 100– 1½" x 9"

**Rectangle 2:** Cut 100– 1½" x 11½"

**Rectangle 3:** Cut 100– 1" x 12"

**Rectangle 4:** Cut 100– 1" x 13½"

**Short Connector 5:** Cut 56– ¾" x 14"

**Long Connector 6:** Cut 8– ¾" x 100½"

*See diagrams on this page and next two pages*

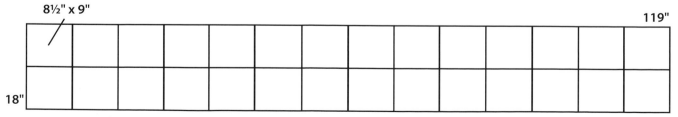

8½" x 9"

119"

18"

**Cutting diagram for Cotton Theory Batting (18" x 119")**

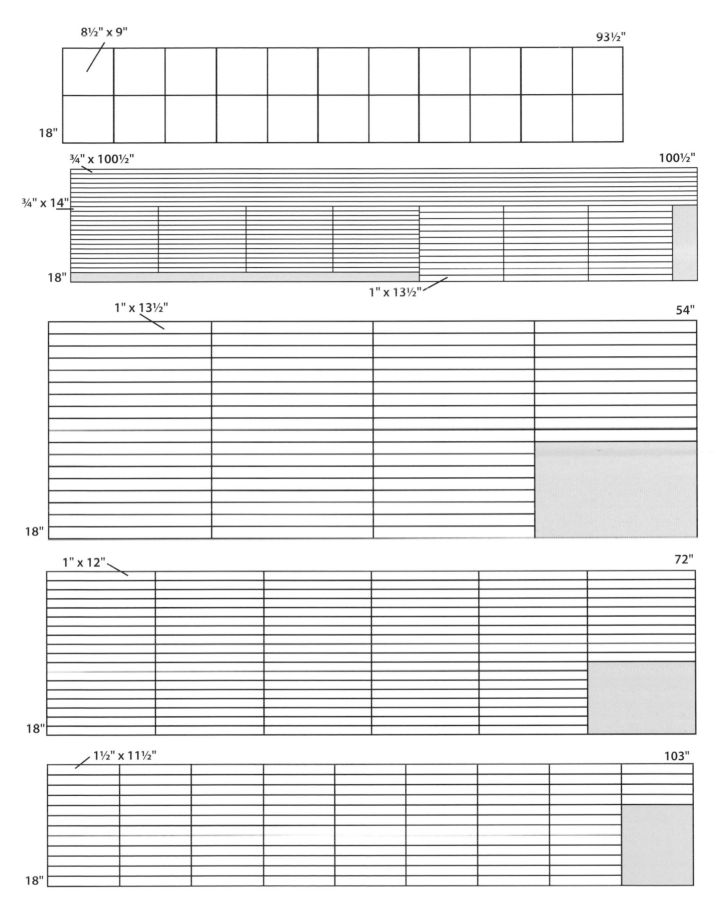

**Cutting diagrams for Cotton Theory Batting (18" x 93½", 18" x 100½", 18" x 54", 18" x 72", and 18" x 103")**

*(Gray area denotes batting that is not used)*

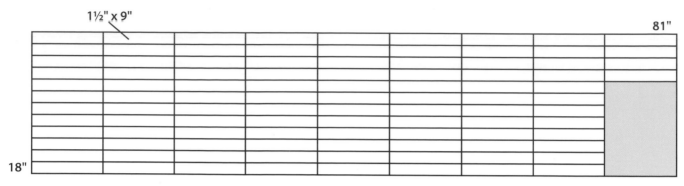

1½" x 9"

81"

18"

**Cutting diagram for Cotton Theory Batting (18" x 81")**
*(Gray area denotes batting that is not used)*

## Quilting Instructions

Insert quilting needle size 90/14 into sewing machine. For best results, use a walking foot when quilting layers.

### Embroidered Blocks

**Note:** Instead of embroidering by hand, you can machine embroider blocks with simple outlines of your choice. When choosing this option, skip Step 1, complete steps 2 and 3, and then machine embroider through all layers. Skip Step 4, because machine embroidery does the quilting.

**1.** Embroider front-side 10½" x 11" blocks by hand as desired.

**Suggested embroidery:** Aunt Martha's Hot Iron Transfers, Design 626, State Birds. Available through the Quilt Yard, Osseo, Wisconsin; phone (715) 597-2452 or (800) 673-8075.

**2.** Layer fabric and batting. Place back-side block right side down, batting in center, and front-side Embroidered Block right side up.

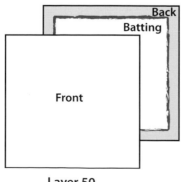

Layer 50

**3.** Press layers together with steam.

**Stitch suggestion:** Straight stitch 2.0 mm long.

**Thread suggestion:** Match thread to the fabric for each side.

**4.** Using a small running stitch, quilt around the outside of each bird motif about ⅛" from hand embroidery.

**Red dotted line indicates quilting**

**Optional quilting:** Echo quilt additional rows from previous quilting to cover the remainder of the block.

### Half-Square Triangles

**1.** Mark a diagonal line on wrong side of 3½" x 3½" squares.

**2.** With right sides together, place squares in all four corners on front of Embroidered Blocks. Diagonal line should cross each corner, as shown in diagram on next page.

**56**

## Stitch suggestion:
Straight stitch 3.5 mm long.

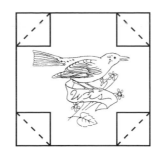

3. Sew on diagonal lines, through all layers.

4. Trim the squares and front-side fabric ¼" from diagonal lines, as shown in diagram. (Do not cut batting.)

**Note:** If you echo quilted the entire block, you won't be able to trim the front-side fabric. Just trim the squares.

5. Press triangles into corners, as shown in diagram.

Sew 50

## Rectangles 1 and 2

1. Layer back fabric right side down, batting in center, and front fabric right side up.

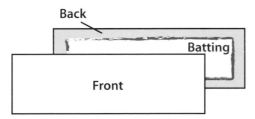

Back
Batting
Front

2. Press layers together with steam.

**Stitch suggestion:** Zigzag 0.5 mm wide and 3.0 mm long (wobble stitch).

3. Place Adhesive Quilting Guide 1¾" to right of sewing machine needle to provide a straight quilting row.

4. Quilt down the middle of Rectangles 1 and 2. (Quilt through entire length of rectangles.)

1¾"

Quilt 100 of Rectangles 1 and 2

5. Using edge of presser foot as a guide, quilt one row on each side of the middle (total of three rows).

## Rectangles 3 and 4

1. Layer back fabric right side down, batting in center, and front fabric right side up.

2. Press layers together with steam.

3. Place Adhesive Quilting Guide 1⅜" to right of sewing machine needle.

4. Quilt down long sides of Rectangles 3 and 4 (total of two rows per rectangle).

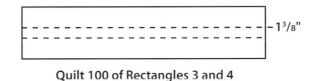

1³/8"

Quilt 100 of Rectangles 3 and 4

## Short Connector 5 and Long Connector 6

1. Layer back fabric right side down, batting in center, and front fabric right side up.

2. Press layers together with steam.

3. Place Adhesive Quilting Guide 1⅜" to right of sewing machine needle.

4. Quilt one row down the middle of Short Connector 5 and Long Connector 6.

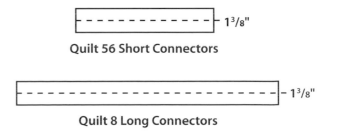

1³/8"

Quilt 56 Short Connectors

1³/8"

Quilt 8 Long Connectors

# Assembly Instructions

Insert topstitch needle size 90/14 into sewing machine.

Seam allowances will be finished on front side of project using the One-Way Street™ procedure, described in Techniques chapter.

**Note:** Use a 1" seam allowance when sewing your quilted pieces together.

**Thread suggestion:** 40-weight green variegated cotton on top and 40-weight pink variegated cotton in bobbin.

**Stitch suggestion:** Straight stitch 3.5 mm long; joining stitch 6.0 mm wide and 4.0 mm long.

## Embroidered Blocks

1. With back sides together (back fabrics against each other) and using a 1" seam, sew Rectangle 1 to sides of

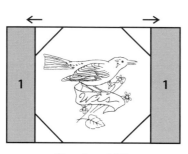

Construct 50

Embroidered Blocks. Stitch through all layers.

2. Press the back side; then press all seam allowances on front side toward Rectangle 1.

3. Finish seams using the One-Way Street procedure, explained in Techniques chapter.

4. With back sides together and using a 1" seam, sew Rectangle 2 to top and bottom of Embroidered Blocks.

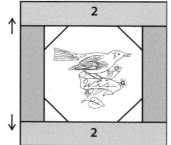

Construct 50

5. Press the back side; then press all seam allowances on front side toward Rectangle 2.

6. Finish seams using the One-Way Street procedure.

7. With back sides together, sew Rectangle 3 to sides of Embroidered Blocks.

8. Press all seam allowances on front side toward Rectangle 3.

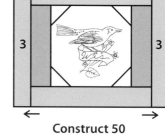

Construct 50

9. Finish seams using the One-Way Street procedure.

10. With back sides together, sew Rectangle 4 to top and bottom of Embroidered Blocks.

11. Press all seam allowances on front side toward Rectangle 4.

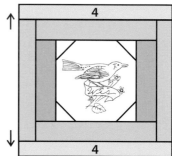

Construct 50

12. Finish seams using the One-Way Street procedure.

## Short Connectors

*Short Connectors will join the Embroidered Blocks into rows.*

**Note:** Forty-nine Embroidered Blocks are used to assemble this quilt. Save your favorite 50th block to make a matching pillow, following instructions in next chapter of this book.

**Betty's Advice:** *Use the Cotton Theory Adhesive Quilting Guide for accurate seam allowances.*

1. Arrange seven rows of Embroidered Blocks with seven blocks in each row (total of 49 blocks), as shown in quilt diagram at end of this chapter.

2. With back sides together and using a 1" seam, sew Short Connector 5 to right-hand side of 49 Embroidered Blocks.

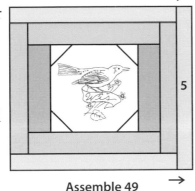

Assemble 49

3. Press all seam allowances on front side toward Short Connector 5.

4. Finish seams using the One-Way Street procedure.

5. With back sides together and using a 1" seam, join one block to another by sewing right-hand side of Short Connector 5 to left side of an Embroidered Block.

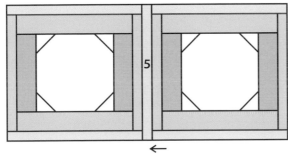

6. Press all seam allowances on front side toward Short Connector 5.

7. Finish seams using the One-Way Street procedure.

**Note:** The finished size of Short Connector 5 will be ¾". After you fold and topstitch the right-hand and left-hand seam allowances, the actual connector will be hidden beneath the folds. This is called Merging Lanes.

8. Continue joining blocks in this manner until there are seven blocks in each row and you have a total of seven rows.

9. With back sides together, sew a Short Connector 5 to the left side of each row, as indicated in diagram at bottom of page.

10. Press all seam allowances on front side toward Short Connector 5.

11. Finish seams using the One-Way Street procedure.

## Long Connectors

*Long Connectors will join together the finished rows.*

1. With back sides together and using a 1" seam, sew Long Connector 6 to bottom of each row, as shown in diagram at bottom of page.

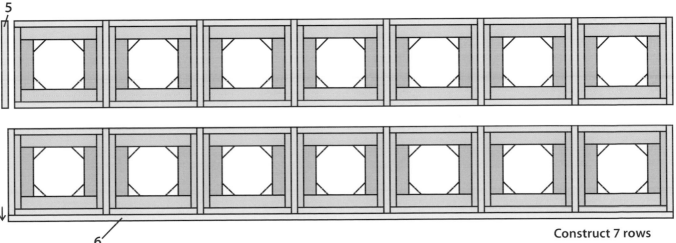

Construct 7 rows

**2.** Press all seam allowances on front side toward Long Connector 6.

**3.** Finish seams using the One-Way Street procedure.

**4.** Align intersections of Short Connectors, as described in Techniques chapter.

**Helpful hint:** When connecting rows, work from bottom to top of your project to keep the quilt from being rolled up in the throat of your sewing machine.

**5.** With back sides together and starting with bottom rows, join rows together. Finish with One-Way Street procedure.

**6.** With back sides together, sew Long Connector 6 to top of quilt, as indicated in diagram, and finish with the One-Way Street procedure.

## Binding

**1.** Trim ⅝" from raw edges of quilt, leaving a ⅜" seam allowance on all sides.

**2.** Apply French-Fold Binding. (For instructions, see Binding chapter near end of this book.)

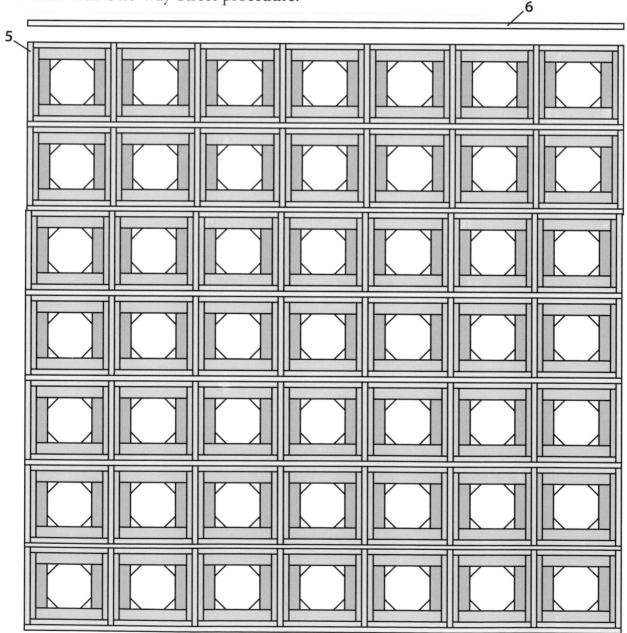

**Front of Feathered Fling Quilt**

60

# Feathered Fling Pillow

### (16½" x 17")

This simple pillow was created using one hand-embroidered block left over after construction of the Feathered Fling Quilt. The block features Aunt Martha's Hot Iron Transfers, Design 626, State Birds. The design is available through the Quilt Yard, Osseo, Wisconsin; phone (715) 597-2452 or (800) 673-8075. You can choose a different embroidery design, if you wish, or you can machine embroider your block with a simple outline of your choice.

**Basic block:** 1– 8½" x 9" embroidered block (10½" x 11" unfinished)

**Project features:**

■ Hand-done embroidery
■ One-Way Street™ procedure

## Yardage Requirements

*Based on 42-inch wide fabric*

> **Note:** If you have constructed the Feathered Fling Quilt, you already have an embroidered, quilted, and assembled block for this pillow. You only need fabric and batting for Rectangles 5 and 6 (front side and back side) and for the pillow's envelope-style enclosure.

### Front Side

**Block for Embroidery:** 1– 10½" x 11" cream

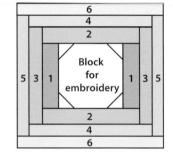

**Half-Square Triangles:** 4– 3½" x 3½" soft gold

**Rectangle 1:** 2– 3½" x 11" dark pink

**Rectangle 2:** 2– 3½" x 13½" dark green

**Rectangle 3:** 2– 3" x 14" medium pink

**Rectangle 4:** 2– 3" x 15½" medium green

**Rectangle 5:** 2– 2¾" x 16" light pink

**Rectangle 6:** 2– 2¾" x 17" light green

### Back Side (inside of pillow front)

**Back of Block:** 1– 10½" x 11" dark pink print

**Rectangle 1:** 2– 3½" x 11" medium pink

**Rectangle 2:** 2– 3½" x 13½" medium pink

**Rectangle 3:** 2– 3" x 14" cream/pink print

**Rectangle 4:** 2– 3" x 15½" cream/pink print

**Rectangle 5:** 2– 2¾" x 16" cream

**Rectangle 6:** 2– 2¾" x 17" cream

### Back Envelope-Style Enclosure

2– 17" x 20" light pink rectangles

### Batting

Cotton Theory Batting, 18" x 25"

### Other Supplies

1– 16" x 16" pillow form

## Batting Cutting Instructions

Cut longest pieces of batting first. Please label your cut pieces.

**Embroidered Block:** Cut 1– 8½" x 9"

**Rectangle 1:** Cut 2– 1½" x 9"

**Rectangle 2:** Cut 2– 1½" x 11½"

**Rectangle 3:** Cut 2– 1" x 12"

**Rectangle 4:** Cut 2– 1" x 13½"

**Rectangle 5:** Cut 2– 1½" x 14"

**Rectangle 6:** Cut 2– 1½" x 16½"

**Cutting diagram for Cotton Theory Batting (18" x 25")**
*(Gray area denotes batting that is not used)*

## Quilting Instructions

Insert quilting needle size 90/14 into sewing machine. For best results, use a walking foot when quilting layers.

If you already have an embroidered, quilted, and assembled block left over from construction of the Feathered Fling Quilt, you can proceed to the instructions for Rectangles 5 and 6 on this page.

If you are making this pillow from the beginning, please quilt the pieces for one block by following the step-by-step instructions on Pages 56 and 57 of Feathered Fling Quilt. Complete the steps for Embroidered Block, Half-Square Triangles, and Rectangles 1, 2, 3, and 4. Then return to this page, and proceed with Rectangles 5 and 6.

### Rectangles 5 and 6

**Note:** Batting for Rectangles 5 and 6 is positioned differently from other rectangles.

1. Place back-side fabric right side down, and position batting 1" from raw edge on one long side, as shown in diagram. (Batting will stop ¼" from other long side.)

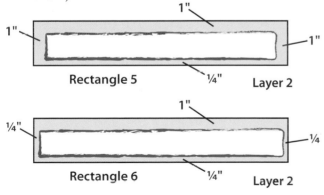

2. Place front-side fabric right side up on top of batting and back-side fabric.

3. Press layers together with steam.

4. Place Adhesive Quilting Guide 1⅜" to right of sewing machine needle.

5. Quilt one row down long side that has no batting within 1" of raw edge.

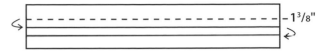

6. Using edge of presser foot as a guide, quilt two more rows toward other long side of Rectangles 5 and 6 (total of three rows).

## Assembly Instructions

Insert topstitch needle size 90/14 into sewing machine.

Seam allowances will be finished on front side of pillow using the One-Way Street™ procedure, described in Techniques chapter.

**Note:** Use a 1" seam allowance when sewing your quilted pieces together.

**Thread suggestion:** 40-weight green variegated cotton on top and 40-weight pink variegated cotton in bobbin.

**Stitch suggestion:** Straight stitch 3.5 mm long; joining stitch 6.0 mm wide and 4.0 mm long.

**Important note:** If you already have an assembled block left over from construction of the Feathered Fling Quilt, please proceed to the instructions for Rectangles 5 and 6 on the next page.

If you are making this pillow from the beginning, please follow the assembly instructions on Page 58 of Feathered Fling Quilt. Assemble one block by completing the steps for the Embroidered Block and Rectangles 1, 2, 3, and 4. Then return to this chapter, and proceed with the assembly instructions for Rectangles 5 and 6 on the next page.

## Rectangles 5 and 6

**Note:** The long side that has no batting within 1" of raw edge will be sewn to the quilted block.

1. With back sides together, sew Rectangle 5 to sides of block.

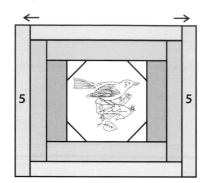

2. Press all seam allowances on front side toward Rectangle 5.

3. Finish seams using the One-Way Street procedure.

4. With back sides together, sew Rectangle 6 to top and bottom of block.

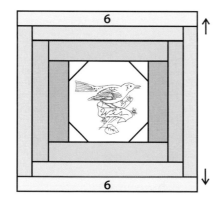

5. Press all seam allowances on front side toward Rectangle 6.

6. Finish seams using the One-Way Street procedure.

## Applying Backing

**Note:** The backing for this pillow is constructed in an envelope style, with one side overlapping the other.

1. With wrong sides together, fold the two backing rectangles in half. (Each folded rectangle should measure 17" x 10".)

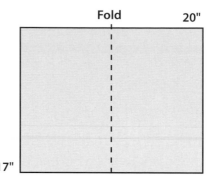

2. Pin the folded rectangles to front side of pillow block, with raw edges even and with folded edges toward the middle. (Folded rectangles will overlap.)

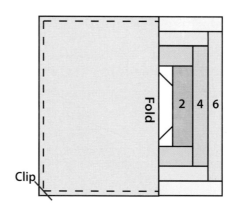

**This diagram shows one folded rectangle. The second folded rectangle will cover the remainder of the pillow block and overlap the first rectangle.**

3. Using a ¼" seam, sew around entire pillow block.

4. Clip corners diagonally.

5. Turn pillow cover right side out.

6. Insert 16" x 16" pillow form.

# Quick Step Banner

(19½" x 45")

**Front side of Quick Step Banner**

**Back side of Quick Step Banner**

*You can give this banner a scrappy look by using different cream, pink, and green print fabrics for the top and bottom basket blocks, as shown in this photo, or you can achieve a more formal look by using the same fabrics for both blocks.*

## Project features:

- Blocks with setting triangles
- Back-to-back blocks
- Back-to-back embroidery
- One-Way Street™ procedure
- Freeway™ procedure on border

## Basic blocks:

2– 9" x 9" Basket Blocks
(9½" x 9½"unfinished)

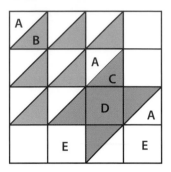

2– 9" x 9" Square-in-Square Blocks
(9½" x 9½" unfinished)

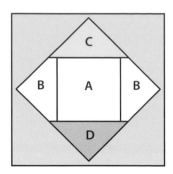

## Yardage Requirements

*Based on 42-inch wide fabric*

### Front Side

**Basket Blocks:**

*Yardage requirements are based on using the same fabrics for both Basket Blocks. If you prefer a scrappy look, divide each yardage total accordingly.*

**A and E:** Total of ¼ yd. cream

**B:** ⅛ yd. pink

**C and D:** Total of ⅛ yd. green

**Setting Triangles:** ⅜ yd. second cream fabric

**Center Rectangle, Bottom Rectangle and Casing:** Total of ⅝ yd. second cream fabric

**Border:** ½ yd. green

### Back Side

**Square-in-Square Blocks:**

**A:** ¼ yd. snowman novelty print

**B:** ¼ yd. cream (same as second cream fabric on front side)

**C:** ¼ yd. blue

**D:** ¼ yd. red check

**Setting Triangles:** ⅜ yd. red/green plaid

**Center Rectangle:** Red fat quarter

**Bottom Rectangle:** Red check fat quarter (same fabric as D)

**Border:** ½ yd. cream (same as second cream fabric on front side)

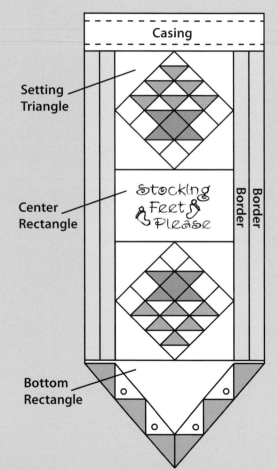

### Binding

¼ yd. cream (same as second cream fabric on front side)

### Batting

Cotton Theory Batting, 18" x 1¾ yd.

## Other Supplies

4– ⅝" cream buttons, 1– 22" quilt hanger

# Fabric Cutting Instructions

Cut carefully to ensure you have an adequate amount of fabric. Label your cut pieces for each side of the project.

## Front Side

**Basket Blocks:**

    **A (cream):** Cut 10– 3⅛" x 3⅛"

    **B (pink):** Cut 6– 3⅛" x 3⅛"

    **C (green):** Cut 4– 3⅛" x 3⅛"

    **D (green):** Cut 2– 2¾" x 2¾"

    **E (cream):** Cut 10– 2¾" x 2¾"

**From second cream fabric:**

    **Setting Triangles:**
Cut 4– 9" x 9"
Cut each in half diagonally

    **Center Rectangle:**
Cut 1– 15½" x 9"

    **Bottom Rectangle:**
Cut 1– 19½" x 11½"

    **Casing:** Cut 1– 20" x 13½"

**Border (green):**
Cut 4– 3½" x 34½"

## Back Side

**Square-in-Square Blocks:**

    **A (snowman print):**
Cut 2– 6¼" x 6¼"

    **B (second cream fabric):**
Cut 2– 7½" x 7½"
Cut each in half diagonally

    **C (blue):**
Cut 1– 7½" x 7½"
Cut square in half diagonally

    **D (red check):**
Cut 1– 7½" x 7½"
Cut square in half diagonally

**Setting Triangles (red/green plaid):**
Cut 4– 9" x 9"
Cut each in half diagonally

**Center Rectangle (red):** Cut 1– 15½" x 9"

**Bottom Rectangle (red check):**
Cut 1– 19½" x 11½"

**Border (second cream fabric):**
Cut 4– 3½" x 34½"

## Binding

Cut 3– 2½" x 42" strips

# Batting Cutting Instructions

Cut longest pieces of batting first. Please label your cut pieces.

**Block:** Cut 2– 13" x 13"

**Center Rectangle:** Cut 1– 6½" x 13"

**Bottom Rectangle:** Cut 1– 10½" x 19½"

**Casing:** Cut 1– 3" x 19"

**Border:** Cut 4– 1½" x 32½"

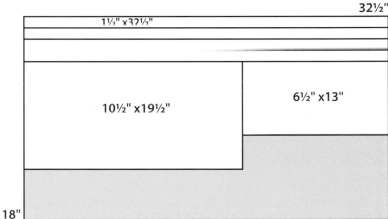

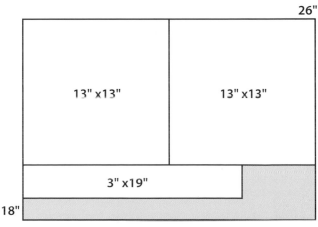

**Cutting diagrams for Cotton Theory Batting
(18" x 32½" and 18" x 26")**
*(Gray area denotes batting that is not used)*

67

## Piecing Instructions

Insert universal size 80/12 needle into sewing machine.

### Front-Side Basket Blocks

1. Mark a diagonal line on wrong side of square A (3⅛" x 3⅛").

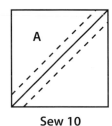

2. With right sides together, place six A squares on B squares (3⅛" x 3⅛"), and place remaining A squares on C squares (3⅛" x 3⅛").

3. Sew a ¼" seam on both sides of the diagonal line on square A, as shown in diagram.

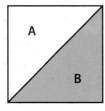

Sew 10

4. Cut on diagonal line. (This will yield two half-square triangles.)

5. Press seams open.

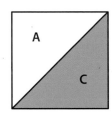

Press 12          Press 8

6. Arrange half-square triangles in the order shown in diagram below.

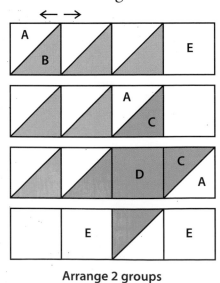

Arrange 2 groups

7. With right sides together, sew half-square triangles together into horizontal rows with a ¼" seam.

8. Press seams open.

9. Sew rows together with ¼" seam to complete two Basket Blocks.

10. Press seams open.

### Front-Side Setting Triangles

**Note:** Setting Triangles will enlarge the Basket Blocks and provide wider seam allowances.

1. With right sides together, sew Setting Triangles to two sides of Basket Blocks with a ¼" seam. (Points of Setting Triangle will extend 1¾" to 2" beyond edges of block.)

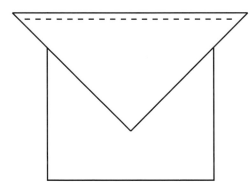

2. Press seam allowances toward triangles.

3. Sew two remaining Setting Triangles to Basket Blocks with a ¼" seam.

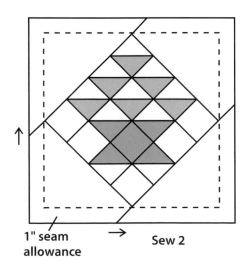

1" seam allowance          Sew 2

4. Press seam allowances toward triangles.

5. Enlarged block should measure 15" x 15".

## Back-Side Square-in-Square Blocks

1. With right sides together, sew B to sides of center square A with a ¼" seam. (Points of B will extend 1¾" to 2" beyond edges of square A.)

2. Press seam allowances toward B.

3. Sew C and D to top and bottom of center square A in same manner. (If center square is a directional print, sew C to top of first center square and to bottom of second center square. Sew D to remaining bottom and top.)

4. Press seam allowances toward C and D.

5. Trim Square-in-Square Blocks to 9½" x 9½"

6. Add Setting Triangles in same manner as you did on Basket Blocks.

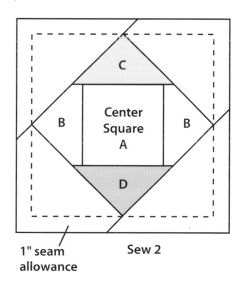

1" seam allowance     Sew 2

7. Press seam allowances toward triangles.

8. Enlarged block should measure 15" x 15".

## Quilting Instructions

Insert quilting needle size 90/14 into sewing machine. For best results, use a walking foot when quilting layers.

### Blocks

1. Place Square-in-Square Block right side down, place batting in center, and place Basket Block right side up. (Make sure Basket Blocks and Square-in-Square Blocks are positioned in direction you want them before quilting.)

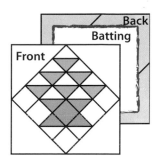

2. Press layers together with steam.

3. Pin to secure layers for quilting.

**Thread suggestion:** 50-weight beige cotton on top and 50-weight light gray cotton in bobbin.

**Stitch suggestion:** Zigzag stitch 0.5 mm wide and 3.0 mm long (wobble stitch).

4. Using wobble stitch and starting at seam of Setting Triangle on Basket Block, quilt in the ditch along first row of Basket Block, then pivot, travel in Setting Triangle seam, and quilt another row one presser-foot width away from previous quilting.

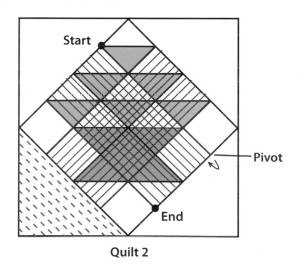

Quilt 2

**69**

**5.** Using edge of presser foot as a guide, quilt approximately 11 additional rows, as shown in diagram on previous page, ending along last row of Basket Block.

**Note:** Because presser-foot widths vary, the number of quilting rows may vary.

**6.** Repeat steps 4 and 5 in crosswise direction, quilting same number of rows.

**7.** Using edge of presser foot as a guide, channel quilt the Setting Triangles, as shown in diagram on previous page. There should be approximately 11 rows in each of the four Setting Triangles.

## Center Rectangle

**1.** Embroider centers for front side and back side of banner as desired.

### Suggested front-side embroidery:
Words "Stocking Feet Please" in a font of your choice. Footprints beside words are OESD, Inc., Left Foot Print NV258 and OESD, Inc., Right Foot Print NV257. Available online from Oklahoma Embroidery Supply & Design, Inc.,  at www.EmbroideryOnline.com.

### Suggested back-side embroidery: Words
"Let It Snow, Let It Snow, Let It Snow" in a font of your choice. Large snowflakes are from Cactus Punch Volume 45, Adventures  In Fleece, Snowflake 4 and Snowflake 1. Available through the Quilt Yard; phone (715) 597-2452 or (800) 673-8075. (Tiny snowflakes are part of quilting described in steps that follow.)

**2.** Layer back rectangle right side down, batting in center, and front rectangle right side up. (Embroidered centers should be back to back with batting between them.)

**3.** Press layers together with steam.

**4.** Select a decorative stitch that resembles tiny snowflakes, similar to samples shown here.

**5.** Push straight pins through all layers to find areas on both sides where embroidered items do not overlap.

Examples of snowflake stitches

**6.** Using a light-colored thread on top and in bobbin, quilt tiny snowflakes in these areas.

## Border

**Thread suggestion:** Match thread to fabric for each side.

**1.** Layer back-side fabric right side down, batting in center, and front fabric right side up.

**2.** Press layers together with steam.

**3.** Place Adhesive Quilting Guide 1⅜" to right of sewing machine needle to provide a straight quilting row.

**4.** Using wobble stitch, quilt down each side of borders, 1⅜" from raw edge. (Quilt through entire length of borders.)

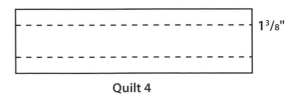

Quilt 4

### Bottom Rectangle

**Thread suggestion:** Match thread to fabric for each side.

1. Layer back-side fabric right side down, batting in center, and front fabric right side up.

**Note:** Batting will be even with raw edges on short sides and bottom of rectangle.

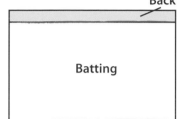

2. Press layers together with steam.

3. Place Adhesive Quilting Guide 1⅜" to right of sewing machine needle.

4. Quilt one row 1⅜" from raw edge.

5. Using edge of presser foot as a guide, channel quilt approximately 25 rows, alternating directions to compensate for fabric shifting. (Quilt until you are about ½" from other raw edge.)

## Assembly Instructions

Insert topstitch needle size 90/14 into sewing machine.

Seam allowances will be 1" and will be finished on front side of banner.

**Thread suggestion:** Match thread to fabric for each side.

**Stitch suggestion:** Straight stitch 3.5 mm long; joining stitch 6.0 mm wide and 4.0 mm long.

### Blocks

1. With back sides together (back fabrics against each other) and using a 1" seam, sew Center Rectangle to bottom of one Basket Block. Stitch through all layers.

2. Press the back side; then press all seam allowances on front side toward Center Rectangle.

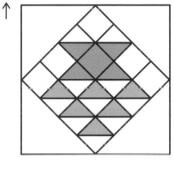

3. Finish seams using the One-Way Street procedure, explained in Techniques chapter.

4. With back sides together and using a 1" seam, sew second Basket Block to Center Rectangle, paying special attention to direction of Basket Block.

5. Press the back side; then press all seam allowances on front side toward Center Rectangle.

6. Finish seams using the One-Way Street procedure.

### Borders

**Note:** The Freeway procedure is used to construct the borders. This procedure is optional and can be replaced by the Highway procedure. Both are explained in the Techniques chapter.

1. With back sides together, sew long side of two Border pieces together with a 1" seam.

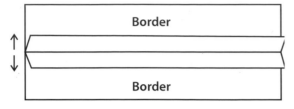

**Construct 2**

2. Press seam open on front side; then press the back side.

**Note:** Look at fabric colors while seam is pressed open. If you want back-side fabric to show on front side of banner, finish the seam using the Freeway procedure. If you don't want back-side fabric to show on front, use the Highway procedure.

3. Finish seam using Freeway or Highway procedure, explained in Techniques chapter.

## Attaching Borders and Bottom Rectangle

1. With back sides together, sew Border sections to long sides of banner with a 1" seam.

2. Press back side; then press all seam allowances on front side toward Borders.

3. Finish seams using the One-Way Street procedure.

4. With back sides together and using a 1" seam, sew long side of Bottom Rectangle to bottom of banner, as shown in diagram in next column.

5. Press the back side; then press all seam allowances on front side toward Bottom Rectangle.

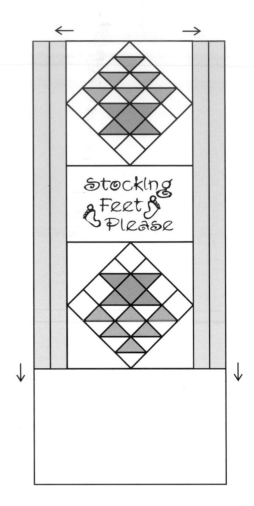

6. Finish seam using the One-Way Street procedure.

## Applying Binding

**Note:** Binding needs to be sewn in place before casing is attached.

1. Trim ⅝" from raw edges of sides and bottom of banner, leaving a ⅜" seam allowance. (Do not trim top edge.)

2. Starting at upper left corner, apply binding to the three trimmed edges, as shown in diagram on next page. There should be no binding on top edge. (For application instructions, see French-Fold Binding in the Binding chapter near end of this book.)

## Folding Bottom Rectangle

1. After binding has been applied, fold up corners of Bottom Rectangle so they meet in the middle, and press them in place.

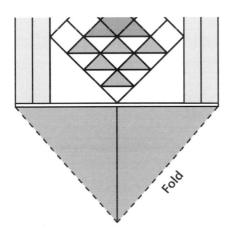

2. Fold portion of corners down so that outside edge of folded portion is even with Border seam, as shown in diagram.

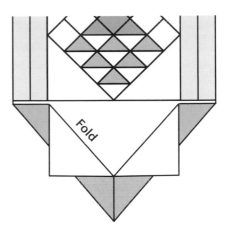

3. Press with steam.

4. Fold corners up again so that points are even with previous fold, as shown in diagram.

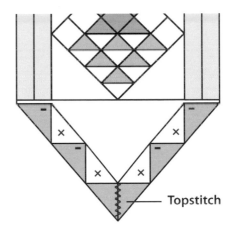

5. Press with steam.

6. Sew buttons through all layers at spots marked by X on diagram.

7. Topstitch the bottom point with a joining stitch, as shown in diagram.

8. Bar tack through all layers, as marked by dash (–) on diagram.

## Preparing and Attaching Casing

1. With right sides together, fold Casing in half so it measures 20" x 6¾".

2. Sew short sides together with a ¼" seam.

3. Clip folded corners, and press seams open.

4. Place batting near folded edge, as shown in diagram.

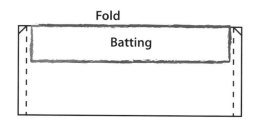

5. Pin batting to one layer of fabric.

6. Turn Casing right side out, and press with steam.

7. Place Adhesive Quilting Guide to the right of the sewing machine needle to quilt the following five rows through all layers of Casing: ⅜", ¾", 1⅛", 1⅞", 2¼".

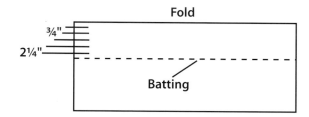

8. With back sides together, sew raw edges of Casing to top of banner with a 1" seam.

9. Press the back side; then press seam allowances on front side toward Casing.

10. Trim seam to ¼".

11. Fold Casing to the original seam on front of banner, covering the trimmed seam allowance, and stitch in place with a joining stitch.

12. Sew the following measurements, as shown in diagram, to complete the Casing: ⅜" from top edge and 1½" from top edge.

13. Insert quilt hanger.

**Suggested quilt hanger:** 22" Flower Garden design from Classic Motifs by Ackfeld Manufacturing. Available through the Quilt Yard; phone (715) 597-2452 or (800) 673-8075.

**Finished front side of Quick Step Banner (19½" x 45")**

# Ohio Reel Quilt

## (84" x 84")

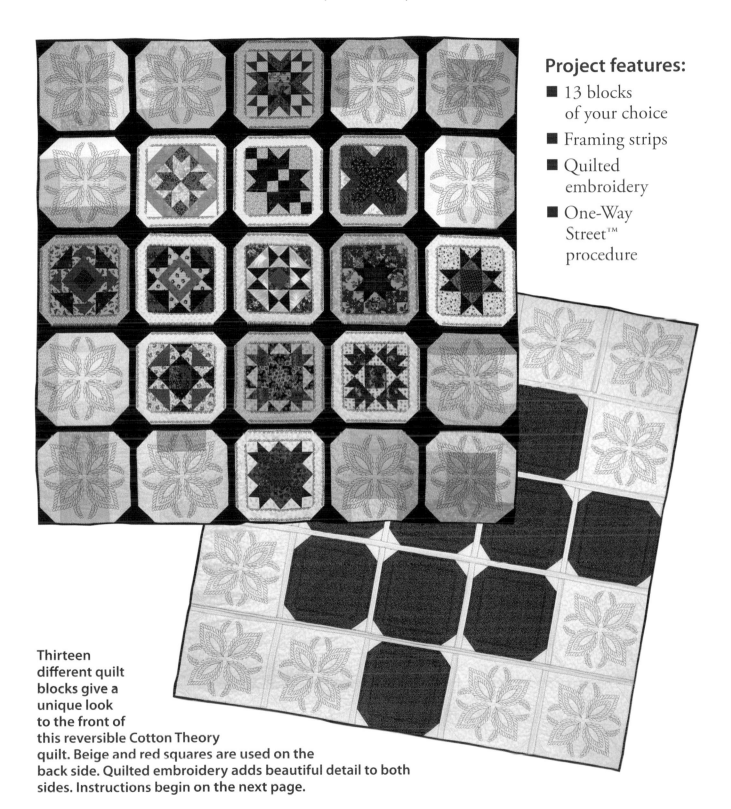

## Project features:

- 13 blocks of your choice
- Framing strips
- Quilted embroidery
- One-Way Street™ procedure

Thirteen different quilt blocks give a unique look to the front of this reversible Cotton Theory quilt. Beige and red squares are used on the back side. Quilted embroidery adds beautiful detail to both sides. Instructions begin on the next page.

*To make this quilt, you need 13 different, pieced blocks, each measuring 12½" x 12½" unfinished. Because these blocks can be any design, their fabric and cutting instructions are not included in this chapter. If you participate in a block-of-the-month program or block exchange, you may want to use those creations in this Ohio Reel Quilt.*

**Basic blocks:** 13– 12" x 12" blocks of your choice (12½" x 12½" unfinished)

## Yardage Requirements

*Based on 42-inch wide fabric*

### Front Side

**Pieced Blocks:** 13 assorted 12" square blocks of your choice (12½" unfinished) *(Yardage not included here)*

**Framing Strips and Background Blocks:** ⅝ yd. each of 13 assorted beige/tan prints

**Half-Square Triangles:** 2 yd. dark red

**Connectors A and B:** 2½ yd. dark red

### Back Side

**Back of Pieced Blocks:** 3¾ yd. red print

**Half-Square Triangles:** 2 yd. first beige

**Background Blocks:** 3¼ yd. second beige

**Connectors A and B:** 2½ yd. first beige

### Binding

¾ yd. dark red

### Batting

Cotton Theory Batting, 18" x 11¼ yd.

## Fabric Cutting Instructions

Cut carefully to ensure you have an adequate amount of fabric. Label your cut pieces for each side of the project.

Where strips are listed, cut them on the crosswise grain (selvage to selvage); then cut sub-cuts from each strip on the lengthwise grain. (See diagrams in Preparation chapter for details.)

### Front Side

**Pieced Blocks (assorted):**
13– 12½" square blocks of your choice

**From each of 13 assorted beige/tan prints:**
    **Framing Strips:**
      Cut 2– 3¼" x 18"
      Cut 2– 3¼" x 12½"

    **Background Blocks:**
      Cut 2– 5" x 18"
      Cut 2– 5" x 9"
      Cut 1– 9" x 9"

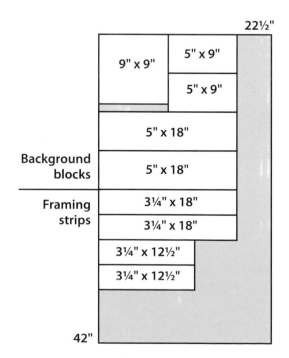

**Fabric cutting diagram for each beige/tan print used for Framing Strips and Background Blocks (42" x 22½")**
*(Gray area denotes fabric that is not used)*

**Half-Square Triangles (dark red):**
Cut 13– 5" strips
Sub-cut 100– 5" x 5"

**Connectors (dark red):**
Cut 1– 86" strip
**Connector B:**
Sub-cut 4– 3" x 86"
**Connector A:**
Sub-cut 20– 3" x 18"

**Back Side**
**Back of Pieced Blocks (red print):**
Cut 7– 18" strips
Sub-cut 13– 18" x 18"

**Half-Square Triangles (first beige):**
Cut 13– 5" strips
Sub-cut 100– 5" x 5"

**Background Blocks (second beige):**
Cut 6– 18" strips
Sub-cut 12– 18" x 18"

**Connectors (first beige):**
Cut 1– 86" strip
**Connector B:**
Sub-cut 4– 3" x 86"
**Connector A:**
Sub-cut 20– 3" x 18"

**Binding**
Cut 9– 2½" x 42" strips

## Batting Cutting Instructions

Cut longest pieces of batting first. Please label your cut pieces.

**Pieced Blocks:** Cut 13– 16" x 16"

**Background Blocks:** Cut 12– 16" x 16"

**Connector A:** Cut 20– 1" x 16"

**Connector B:** Cut 4– 1" x 84"

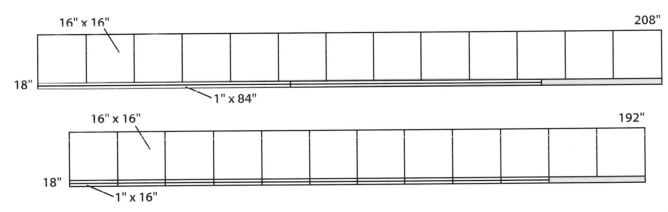

**Cutting diagrams for Cotton Theory Batting (18" x 208" and 18" x 192")** *(Gray area denotes batting that is not used)*

## Piecing Instructions

Insert universal needle size 80/12 into sewing machine.

### Front-Side Pieced Blocks and Framing Strips

*Framing Strips will be sewn to the 13 assorted, pieced blocks. This will provide enlarged seam allowances needed for Cotton Theory construction.*

1.  With right sides together and using a ¼" seam, sew two alike Framing Strips

(3¼" x 12½" to top and bottom of each Pieced Block.

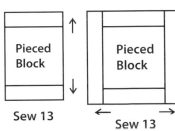

2.  Press seams toward Framing Strips.

3.  With right sides together and using a ¼" seam, sew matching framing strips (3¼" x 18") to sides of each Pieced Block. (All four Framing Strips will be alike for each block.)

4.  Press seams toward Framing Strips.

## Front-Side Background Blocks

*These blocks are meant to be scrappy, with beige and tan prints mixed.*

1. With right sides together and using a ¼" seam, sew two different 5" x 9" rectangles to top and bottom of each 9" x 9" center square.

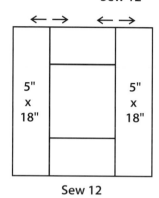

Sew 12

2. Press seams open.

3. With right sides together and using a ¼" seam, sew two different 5" x 18" rectangles to sides of each center.

4. Press seams open.

Sew 12

## Quilting Instructions

Insert quilting needle size 90/14 into sewing machine. For best results, use a walking foot when quilting layers.

### Pieced Blocks

1. Layer fabric and batting. Place back-side block right side down, place batting in center, and place front-side Pieced Block right side up.

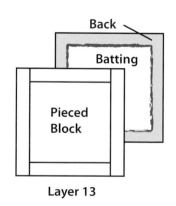

Layer 13

2. Press layers together with steam.

**Stitch suggestion:** Zigzag 0.5 mm wide and 3.0 mm long (wobble stitch).

**Thread suggestion:** Match thread to the fabric for each side.

3. Using wobble stitch, quilt in the ditch on each of the 13 Pieced Blocks. Use needle down and pivot in the seam of Framing Strips. (Do not quilt in the Framing Strips.)

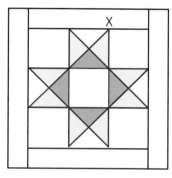

**Betty's Advice:**

*Using a wobble stitch when quilting in the ditch will create an illusion of movement in your blocks.*

Quilt in the ditch on 13 Pieced Blocks. On this block, for example, continuous stitching of eight lines – starting at X, pivoting at each Framing Strip and ending at X – is used to quilt the star.

### Half-Square Triangles

1. With right sides together, place 5" back-side squares (beige) in all four corners on back side of Pieced Blocks.

2. Pin in place through all layers, as shown in diagram.

Pin squares on back side of 13 quilted blocks

**Note:** You will be sewing a diagonal line from front side of block and will not be able to see or remove pins while sewing, so the pins should be positioned as shown in diagram.

3. Turn blocks over.

4. Mark a diagonal line on wrong side of front-side 5" x 5" squares (dark red).

Mark 100

**5.** With right sides together, place 5" front-side squares in all four corners on front side of Pieced Blocks. Position diagonal lines as shown in diagram.

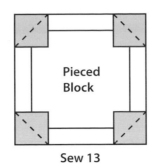

Sew 13

**Stitch suggestion:** Straight stitch 3.5 mm long.

**Note:** You will be sewing the front-side and back-side squares at the same time.

**6.** Sew on front-side diagonal lines, through all layers.

**7.** Trim back-side and front-side squares, back-side block fabric and front-side fabric to ¼" from diagonal seam line, as shown in diagram. (Do not cut batting.)

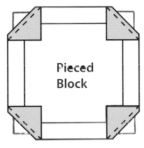

Trim 13 blocks

**8.** Press front-side and back-side triangles into corners, as shown in diagram.

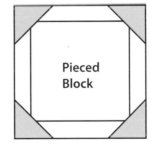

## Decorative Quilting

**Thread suggestion:**
Dark brown 50-weight cotton on top and dark red 50-weight cotton in bobbin.

**1.** Place Adhesive Quilting Guide 1⅜" to right of sewing machine needle.

**2.** Using decorative stitch of your choice, quilt 1⅜"

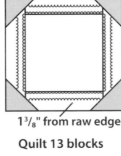

1⅜" from raw edge

Quilt 13 blocks

from raw edges on front side of 13 Pieced Blocks, starting and ending at triangles.

**3.** Using inside edge of presser foot as a guide, quilt with the same decorative stitch along all four Framing Strip seams of Pieced Block.

## Background Blocks

**Suggested embroidery:** Feather design repeated four times on Background Blocks. Design is Anita Goodesigns Quilt Feathers (Mini Collection), Pattern 23C. Available through the Quilt Yard, Osseo, Wisconsin; phone (715) 597-2452 or (800) 673-8075.

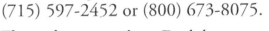

**Thread suggestion:** Dark brown 50-weight cotton on top and dark red 50-weight cotton in bobbin.

**1.** Layer fabric and batting. Place back-side Background Block right side down, place batting in center, and place front-side Background Block right side up.

**2.** Press layers together with steam.

**3.** Place all three layers in machine embroidery hoop, or follow alternate quilting instructions on next page.

**Note:** For machine embroidery, it may be helpful to mark the center of block and place embroidery design in each corner.

**4.** Size embroidery to fit area.

5. Embroider design four times on each Background Block, as shown in diagram.

1" seam allowance

Quilt 12 blocks

**Alternate quilting:** Quilt a diagonal grid, as shown in diagram. Start by quilting a diagonal line from corner to corner; then channel quilt on each side of diagonal line.

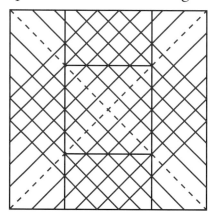

6. With right sides together, place 5" front-side and back-side squares in all four corners on front and back sides of Background Blocks.

7. Pin, sew, trim, and press in same manner as Half-Square Triangles on Pieced Blocks.

1" seam allowance
Sew 12 blocks

## Connectors A and B

1. Layer back-side fabric right side down, batting in center, and front fabric right side up.

2. Press layers together with steam.

3. Place Adhesive Quilting Guide 1⅜" to right of sewing machine needle.

4. Using wobble stitch (zigzag 0.5 mm wide and 3.0 mm long), quilt 1⅜" from raw edges, as shown in diagram. (Quilt through entire length of connectors.)

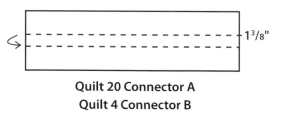

1⅜"

**Quilt 20 Connector A**
**Quilt 4 Connector B**

## Assembly Instructions

Insert topstitch needle size 90/14 into sewing machine.

Seam allowances will be finished on front side of project using the One-Way Street™ procedure, described in Techniques chapter.

**Note:** Use a 1" seam allowance when sewing your quilted pieces together.

**Thread suggestion:** Dark red 50-weight cotton on top and beige 50-weight cotton in bobbin.

**Stitch suggestion:** Straight stitch 3.5 mm long; joining stitch 6.0 mm wide and 4.0 mm long.

### Connector A

1. Refer to quilt diagram at end of this chapter, and arrange blocks for each row.

2. With back sides together (back fabrics against each other) and using a 1" seam, sew Connector A (3" x 18") to right-hand side of first Background Block in first row of quilt. Stitch through all layers.

3. Press the back side; then press all seam allowances on front side toward Connector A.

4. Finish seam using the One-Way Street procedure, explained in Techniques chapter.

5. Continue adding Connector A to right-hand side of first four blocks in each row.

6. Finish each seam using the One-Way Street procedure.

7. With back sides together and using a 1" seam, sew one block to the next block to complete each row.

8. Press all seam allowances on front side toward Connector A.

2. Press seam allowances on front side toward Connector B.

3. Finish seams using the One-Way Street procedure.

## Connecting the Rows

1. Before connecting each row, align intersections of Connector A, as described in Techniques chapter.

2. With back sides together and starting with bottom rows, join rows together, and finish with the One-Way Street procedure. Fold and topstitch each seam before connecting the next row.

# Binding

1. Trim ⅝" from raw edges of project, leaving a ⅜" seam allowance on all sides.

2. Apply binding. (For instructions, see Binding chapter near end of this book.)

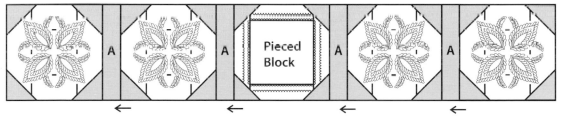

Row 1

9. Finish seams using the One-Way Street procedure.

10. Construct a total of five rows, referring to quilt diagram on next page as needed.

## Connector B

1. With back sides together and using a 1" seam, sew Connector B (3" x 86") to bottom of Rows 1, 2, 3, and 4.

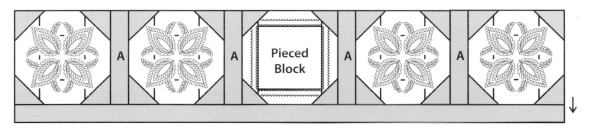

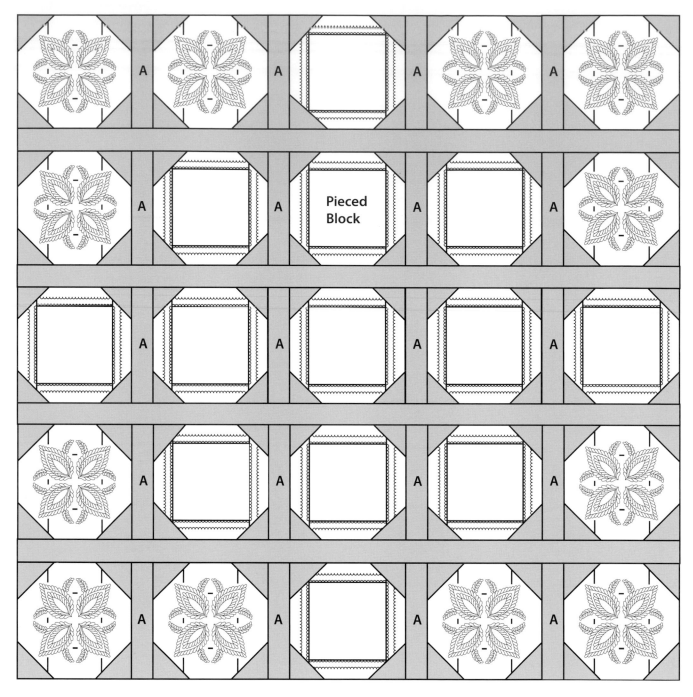

Finished front side of Ohio Reel Quilt

# Log Cabin Shuffle Quilt

(110" x 110")

## Project features:

- 12 blocks of your choice
- Enlarged back-side blocks
- One-Way Street™ procedure

Create this king-size quilt with 24 Log Cabin Blocks and 12 assorted 12-inch blocks of your choice. Three borders finish the quilt beautifully. The back side of this reversible quilt features a window-pane look that has black print squares, salmon tone-on-tone triangles and cream print connectors. Instructions begin on the next page.

To make this quilt, you need 24 Log Cabin Blocks and 12 assorted, pieced blocks, each measuring 12½" x 12½" unfinished.

*Fabric and cutting instructions for the 12 assorted blocks are not included in this chapter.*

*The assorted sampler blocks shown in the photo on the previous page came from a block-of-the-month program.*

**Basic blocks:** 24– 12" x 12" Log Cabin Blocks (12½" x 12½" unfinished)

12– 12" x 12" blocks of your choice (12½" x 12½" unfinished)

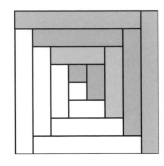

## Yardage Requirements

*Based on 42-inch wide fabric*

### Front Side

**Sampler Blocks:** 12 assorted 12" square blocks of your choice (12½" unfinished) in red, black, cream, and green fabric *(yardage not included here)*

**Log Cabin Blocks:**
   **Center (C):** ¼ yd. first cream print
   **Logs 1 and 2:** ⅜ yd. green print
   **Logs 3 and 4:** ⅝ yd. second cream print
   **Logs 5 and 6:** ¾ yd. red print
   **Logs 7 and 8:** ⅞ yd. third cream print
   **Logs 9 and 10:** 1⅛ yd. second red print
   **Logs 11 and 12:** 1¼ yd. fourth cream print
   **Logs 13 and 14:** 1½ yd. black floral

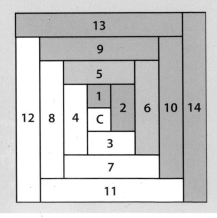

*See diagrams at end of chapter for placement of triangles, connectors, and borders.*

**Half-Square Triangles:** ⅜ yd. green

**Dark Connectors:** 1 yd. black floral

**Light Connectors:**
2 yd. cream tone-on-tone

**First Border:** 2¾ yd. cream tone-on-tone

**Second Border:** 3 yd. green print *(enough yardage for both sides of quilt)*

**Third Border and Binding:** 3¼ yd. black floral

### Back Side

**Back-Side Blocks:** 4¾ yd. black print

**Half-Square Triangles:** ⅜ yd. salmon tone-on-tone

**Connectors:** 2½ yd. cream print

**First Border:** 2¾ yd. cream print

**Second Border:** Green print yardage from front side

**Third Border:** 3¼ yd. red tone-on-tone

### Binding

Black floral (included in Third Border above)

### Batting

Cotton Theory Batting, 18" x 22½ yd.

# Fabric Cutting Instructions

Cut carefully to ensure you have an adequate amount of fabric. Label your cut pieces for each side of the project.

Where strips are listed, cut them on the crosswise grain (selvage to selvage); then cut sub-cuts from each strip on the lengthwise grain. (See diagrams in Preparation chapter for details.)

## Front Side

**Sampler Blocks:**
12– 12½" blocks of your choice in red, black, cream, and green fabric

**Log Cabin Blocks:**

**Center (first cream print):**
Cut 2– 2" strips
Sub-cut 24– 2" x 2"

**Log 1 (green print):**
Cut 2– 2" strips
Sub-cut 24– 2" x 2"

**Log 2 (green print):**
Cut 2– 3½" strips
Sub-cut 24– 2" x 3½"

**Log 3 (second cream print):**
Cut 2– 3½" strips
Sub-cut 24– 2" x 3½"

**Log 4 (second cream print):**
Cut 2– 5" strips
Sub-cut 24– 2" x 5"

**Log 5 (red print):**
Cut 2– 5" strips
Sub-cut 24– 2" x 5"

**Log 6 (red print):**
Cut 2– 6½" strips
Sub-cut 24– 2" x 6½"

**Log 7 (third cream print):**
Cut 2– 6½" strips
Sub-cut 24– 2" x 6½"

**Log 8 (third cream print):**
Cut 2– 8" strips
Sub-cut 24– 2" x 8"

**Log 9 (second red print):**
Cut 2– 8" strips
Sub-cut 24– 2" x 8"

**Log 10 (second red print):**
Cut 2– 9½" strips
Sub-cut 24– 2" x 9½"

**Log 11 (fourth cream print):**
Cut 2– 9½" strips
Sub-cut 24– 2" x 9½"

**Log 12 (fourth cream print):**
Cut 2– 11" strips
Sub-cut 24– 2" x 11"

**Log 13 (black floral):**
Cut 2– 11" strips
Sub-cut 24– 2" x 11"

**Log 14 (black floral):**
Cut 2– 12½" strips
Sub-cut 24– 2" x 12½"

**Half-Square Triangles (green):**
Cut 2– 5" strips
Sub-cut 16– 5" x 5"

**Dark Connectors (black floral):**
Cut 1– 30" strip
**Dark Connector 6B:**
Sub-cut 1– 3½" x 29"
**Dark Connector 2:**
Sub-cut 4– 3½" x 14¾"
**Dark Connector 5:**
Sub-cut 4– 3½" x 14¾"

**Dark Connector 6A:**
Sub-cut 2– 3½" x 14¾"
**Dark Connector 1:**
Sub-cut 4– 3½" x 14"

**Light Connectors (cream tone-on-tone):**
Cut 1– 41" strip
**Light Connector 4:**
Sub-cut 4– 3½" x 41"
**Light Connector 2:**
Sub-cut 4– 3½" x 13¼"
**Light Connector 5:**
Sub-cut 2– 3½" x 12½"
**Light Connector 6:**
Sub-cut 2– 3½" x 12½"

Cut 1– 28" strip
**Light Connector 3:**
Sub-cut 4– 3½" x 27½"
**Light Connector 1:**
Sub-cut 16– 3½" x 14"

**First Border (cream tone-on-tone):**
Cut 1– 93½" strip
Sub-cut 2– 8" x 93½"
Sub-cut 2– 8" x 81½"

**Second Border (green print):**
Cut 1– 99½" strip
*(enough yardage for both sides)*
Sub-cut 2– 5" x 99½"
Sub-cut 2– 5" x 93½"

**Third Border and Binding (black floral):**
Cut 1– 111½" strip
**Third Border:**
Sub-cut 2– 8" x 111½"
Sub-cut 2– 8" x 99½"
**Binding:**
Sub-cut 4– 2½" x 111½"

*More fabric cutting instructions on next page*

## Back Side

**Back-Side Blocks (black print):**
Cut 12– 14" strips
Sub-cut 36– 14" x 14"

**Half-Square Triangles (salmon tone-on-tone):**
Cut 2– 5" strips
Sub-cut 16– 5" x 5"

**Connectors (cream print):**
Cut 1– 83" strip
  **Connector 6:**
  Sub-cut 1– 3½" x 81½"

**Connector 5:**
Sub-cut 2– 3½" x 41"

**Connector 4:**
Sub-cut 4– 3½" x 41"

**Connector 3:**
Sub-cut 4– 3½" x 27½"

**Connector 2:**
Sub-cut 4– 3½" x 27½"

**Connector 1:**
Sub-cut 20– 3½" x 14"

**First Border (cream print):**
Cut 1– 93½" strip
Sub-cut 2– 8" x 93½"
Sub-cut 2– 8" x 81½"

**Second Border (green print):**
Use yardage from front side
Sub-cut 2– 5" x 99½"
Sub-cut 2– 5" x 93½"

**Third Border (red tone-on-tone):**
Cut 1– 111½" strip
Sub-cut 2– 8" x 111½"
Sub-cut 2– 8" x 99½"

# Batting Cutting Instructions

Cut longest pieces of batting first. Please label your cut pieces.

**Blocks:** Cut 36– 12" x 12"

**Connector 1:** Cut 20– 1½" x 12"

**Connector 2:** Cut 4– 1½" x 25½"

**Connector 3:** Cut 4– 1½" x 25½"

**Connector 4:** Cut 4– 1½" x 39"

**Connector 5:** Cut 2– 1½" x 39"

**Connector 6:** Cut 1– 1½" x 79½"

**First Border:**
Cut 2– 6" x 91½"
Cut 2– 6" x 79½"

**Second Border:**
Cut 2– 3" x 97½"
Cut 2– 3" x 91½"

**Third Border:**
Cut 2– 6" x 109½"
Cut 2– 6" x 97½"

*See batting cutting diagrams on this page and next page.*

**Cutting diagrams for Cotton Theory Batting (18" x 91½" and 18" x 79½")**
*(Gray area denotes batting that is not used)*

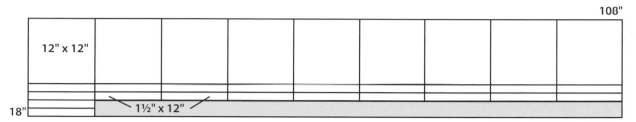

Cut four of these, so you have a total of 36 blocks measuring 12" x 12". The 1½" x 12" cuts are needed on only one of these and can be eliminated on the other three. *(Gray area denotes batting that is not used.)*

| 6" x 109½" |
| 6" x 109½" |
| 6" x 91½" |

| 6" x 97½" |
| 6" x 97½" |
| 3" x 97½" |
| 3" x 97½" |

Cutting diagrams for Cotton Theory Batting (18" x 108", 18" x 109½", and 18" x 97½")
*(Gray area denotes batting that is not used)*

## Piecing Instructions

Insert universal needle size 80/12 into sewing machine.

### Log Cabin Blocks

1. With right sides together and using a ¼" seam, sew Log 1 to top of Center.

2. Press seam allowances toward Log 1.

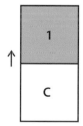

**Sew 24**

3. With right sides together and using a ¼" seam, sew Log 2 to right-hand side of Center unit.

4. Press seam allowances toward Log 2.

**Sew 24**

5. With right sides together, sew Log 3 to bottom of Center unit.

6. Press seam allowances toward Log 3.

7. With right sides together, sew Log 4 to left side of the Center unit.

8. Press seam allowances toward Log 4.

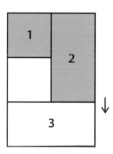

**Sew 24**

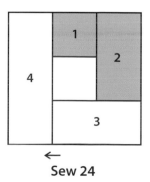

**Sew 24**

**87**

9. With right sides together, sew Log 5 to top of Center unit.

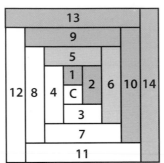

**Sew 24**

10. Press seam allowances toward Log 5.

11. Continue adding Logs 6 through 14 clockwise, pressing after sewing each seam.

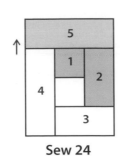

**Sew 24**

## Front-Side Connectors

**Note:** Please label connectors.

1. With right sides together and using a ¼" seam, piece together Dark Connector 2 (3½" x 14¾") and Light Connector 2 (3½" x 13¼"), as shown in diagram, to create front-side Connector 2.

| Dark 2 | Light 2 |
|---|---|

**Make 4 of Connector 2**

2. Press seams open.

3. Piece together Dark Connector 5 (3½" x 14¾"), Light Connector 5 (3½" x 12½"), and Dark Connector 5 (3½" x 14¾") to create front-side Connector 5.

| Dark 5 | Light 5 | Dark 5 |
|---|---|---|

**Make 2 of Connector 5**

4. Press seams open.

5. Piece together Dark Connector 6A (3½" x 14¾"), Light Connector 6 (3½" x 12½"), Dark Connector 6B (3½" x 29"), Light Connector 6 (3½" x 12½"), and Dark Connector 6A (3½" x 14¾") to create front-side Connector 6. Press seams open.

| Dark 6A | Light 6 | Dark 6B | Light 6 | Dark 6A |
|---|---|---|---|---|

**Make 1 of Connector 6**

# Quilting Instructions

Insert quilting needle size 90/14 into sewing machine. For best results, use a walking foot when quilting layers.

**Stitch suggestion:** Zigzag 0.5 mm wide and 3.0 mm long (wobble stitch).

**Thread suggestion:** Match thread to the fabric for each side.

**Note:** It is very important to layer blocks accurately. There is only a ¼" seam allowance on traditional blocks, so there is not much room for variation.

## Sampler Blocks

1. Layer fabric and batting. Place Back-side Block right side down, place batting in center, and place front-side Sampler Block right side up.

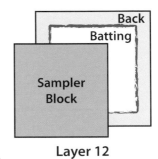

**Layer 12**

**Note:** Because the Back-Side Block has a 1" seam allowance and the Sampler Block has a ¼" seam allowance, the Back-Side Block will be ¾" larger than the front block on all sides.

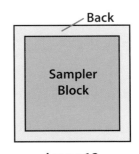

**Layer 12**

2. Press layers together with steam.

3. Pin or baste layers together to help secure them during quilting.

4. Quilt 12 Sampler Blocks as desired, perhaps quilting in the ditch because the blocks vary in design.

## Log Cabin Blocks

**Note:** Half-Square Triangles will be sewn to the light portion of 16 Log Cabin Blocks and to 16 Back-Side Blocks at the same time.

1. With right sides together, place 5" front-side squares (green) on the light corners of 16 Log Cabin Blocks, lining up the outside edges of each square with the back-side fabric.

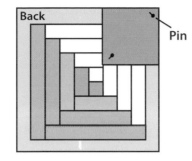

2. Pin in place as indicated in diagram.

3. Mark a diagonal line on wrong side of back-side 5" squares (salmon tone-on-tone).

4. With right sides together, place back-side squares on Back-Side Blocks in same corner as Log Cabin Blocks.

5. Pin in place, through all layers.

6. Sew on diagonal line, through all layers.

7. Trim back-side and front-side squares, Back-Side Block and front-side Log Cabin Block ¼" from diagonal seam line, as shown in diagram. (Do not cut batting.)

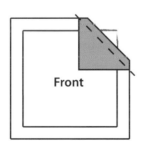

8. Press front-side and back-side triangles into corners. Square up the corners, if necessary.

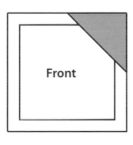

9. Using wobble stitch (zigzag 0.5 mm wide and 3.0 mm long), place right edge of presser foot along edge of front-side triangle and quilt one row in light portion of Log Cabin Block.

10. Continue adding quilt rows, as shown in diagram below, until you reach the dark points of the logs.

**Note:** If your rows are ⅜" apart, you will have about 13 rows.

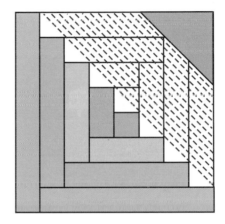

## Connectors 1 through 6

**Thread suggestion:** Match thread to the fabric for each side.

1. Pair up back-side and front-side Connectors 1 through 6. (Some front-side Connector 1 pieces will be dark, and some will be light.)

2. Layer back-side fabric right side down, batting in center, and front fabric right side up.

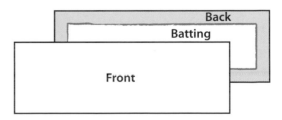

3. Press layers together with steam.

4. Place Adhesive Quilting Guide 1¾" to right of sewing machine needle.

5. Using wobble stitch (zigzag 0.5 mm wide and 3.0 mm long), quilt down the middle of Connectors 1 through 6. (Quilt through entire length of connectors.)

6. Quilt another row one presser-foot width away on both sides of middle (total of three rows).

## First and Third Borders

1. Layer back-side fabric right side down, batting in center, and front fabric right side up.

2. Press layers together with steam.

3. Place Adhesive Quilting Guide 4" to right of sewing machine needle.

4. Using wobble stitch, quilt down the middle of First and Third Borders.

5. Quilt another row one presser-foot width away on both sides of middle (total of three rows).

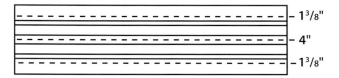

6. Place Adhesive Quilting Guide 1⅜" to right of sewing machine needle.

7. Quilt 1⅜" from raw edges of Connectors 1 through 6.

8. Using edge of presser foot as a guide, quilt two more rows toward the middle, as shown in diagram above.

## Second Border

1. Layer back-side fabric right side down, batting in center, and front fabric right side up.

2. Press layers together with steam.

3. Place Adhesive Quilting Guide 2½" to right of sewing machine needle.

4. Using wobble stitch, quilt down the middle.

5. Channel quilt three more rows one presser-foot width away from previous quilting on both sides of middle (total of seven rows, if your rows are ⅜" apart). Alternate directions while quilting to compensate for fabric shifting.

# Assembly Instructions

*Four sections will be constructed and then assembled into one quilt.*

Insert topstitch needle size 90/14 into sewing machine.

Seam allowances will be finished on front side of this project using the One-Way Street™ procedure, described in Techniques chapter.

**Note:** Use a 1" seam allowance when sewing your quilted pieces together.

**Thread suggestion:** Match thread to the fabric for each side.

**Stitch suggestion:** Straight stitch 3.5 mm long; joining stitch 6.0 mm wide and 4.0 mm long.

1. Refer to block diagram on next page, and arrange the four sections of the quilt, carefully positioning Log Cabin Blocks and Sampler Blocks to match the diagram.

2. Label each block A through I.

3. With back sides together (back fabrics against each other) and using a 1" seam, sew Dark Connector 1 to bottom of two Log Cabin A and to top of two Log Cabin A, paying close attention to light/dark position of Log Cabin Blocks. Sew through all layers.

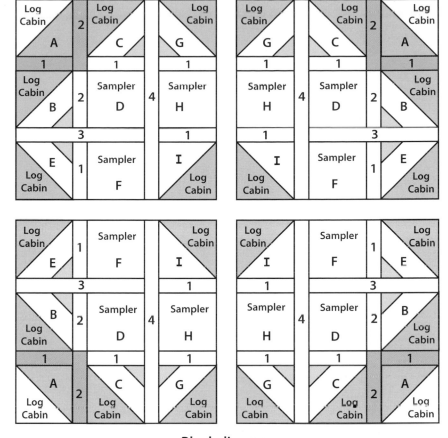

**Block diagram**

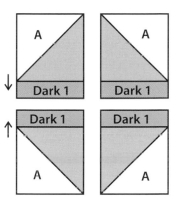

4. Press the back side; then press all seam allowances on front side toward Dark Connector 1.

5. Finish seams using the One-Way Street procedure, explained in Techniques chapter. (Trim one layer, fold two.)

6. With back sides together, sew Log Cabin B to bottom of two Log Cabin A units and to top of two Log Cabin A units, paying close attention to position of Log Cabin B corner triangles.

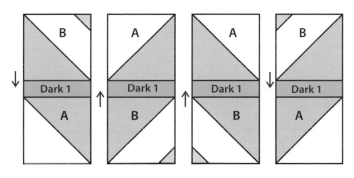

7. Press the back side; then press all seam allowances on front side toward Dark Connector 1.

8. Finish seams using the One-Way Street procedure.

9. With back sides together, sew Light Connector 1 to bottom of two Log Cabin C and to top of two Log Cabin C, paying attention to position of corner triangles.

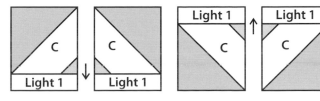

10. Press seam allowances on front side toward Light Connector 1.

11. Finish seams using the One-Way Street procedure.

91

**12.** With back sides together, sew Sampler D to bottom of two Log Cabin C units and to top of two Log Cabin C units, paying attention to position of Log Cabin C triangles.

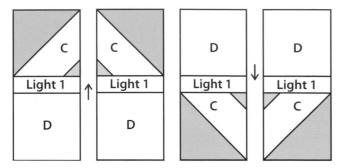

**13.** Press seam allowances on front side toward Light Connector 1.

**14.** Finish seams using the One-Way Street procedure.

**15.** With back sides together, sew Connector 2 (light/dark combination) to left side of two Blocks C/D and to right-hand side of two Blocks C/D, paying attention to position of connectors and blocks. Match up seam lines of Connector 2 and Light Connector 1.

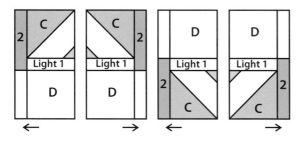

**16.** Press seam allowances on front side toward Connector 2.

**17.** Finish seams using the One-Way Street procedure.

**18.** Align intersections, as described in Techniques chapter. Then sew Block C/D to Block A/B with back sides together, paying close attention to positioning of blocks, as shown in diagram at top of next column.

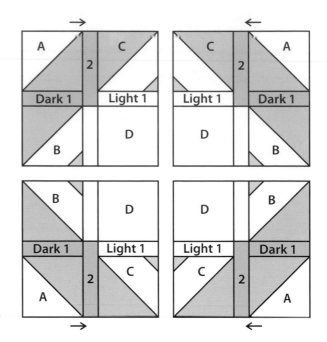

**19.** Press seam allowances on front side toward Connector 2, and finish seams using the One-Way Street procedure.

**20.** With back sides together, sew Light Connector 1 to left side of two Sampler F and to right-hand side of two Sampler F.

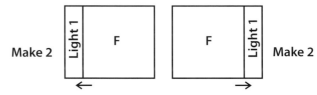

**21.** Press seam allowances on front side toward Light Connector 1, and finish seams using the One-Way Street procedure.

**22.** With back sides together, sew Log Cabin E to Sampler F units, paying attention to position of Log Cabin E corner triangles.

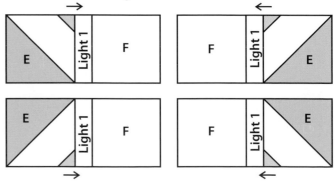

**23.** Press seam allowances on front side toward Light Connector 1, and finish seams using the One-Way Street procedure.

**24.** With back sides together, sew Connector 3 to bottom of two Blocks E/F and to top of two Blocks E/F, paying attention to position of Log Cabin E corner triangles.

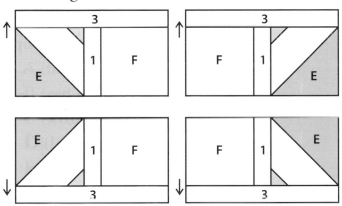

**25.** Press seam allowances on front side toward Connector 3, and finish seams using the One-Way Street procedure.

**26.** With back sides together, sew Block E/F to bottom of two A/B/C/D units and to top of two A/B/C/D units, paying attention to position of corner triangles.

**27.** Press seam allowances on front side toward Connector 3, and finish seams using the One-Way Street procedure.

**28.** With back sides together, sew Light Connector 1 to bottom of two Log Cabin G and to top of two Log Cabin G, paying attention to position of corner triangles.

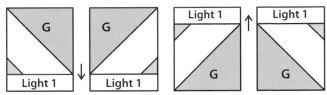

**29.** Press seam allowances on front side toward Light Connector 1, and finish seams using the One-Way Street procedure.

**30.** With back sides together, sew Sampler H to bottom of two Log Cabin G units and to top of two Log Cabin G units, paying attention to position of corner triangles.

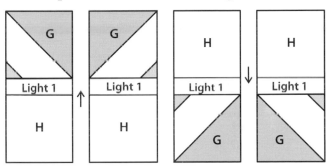

**31.** Press seam allowances on front side toward Light Connector 1, and finish seams using the One-Way Street procedure.

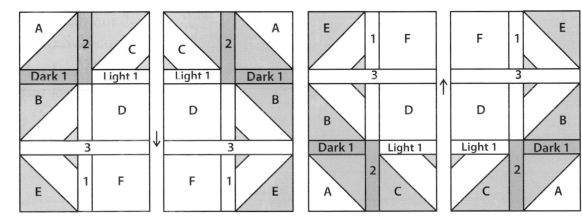

**32.** With back sides together, sew Light Connector 1 to bottom of two Blocks G/H and to top of two Blocks G/H.

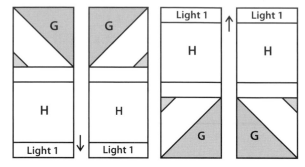

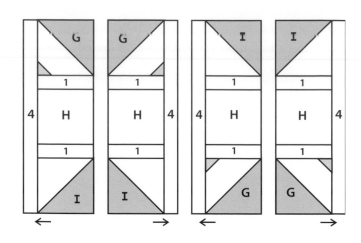

**33.** Press seam allowances on front side toward Light Connector 1, and finish seams using the One-Way Street procedure.

**37.** Press seam allowances on front side toward Connector 4, and finish seams using One-Way Street procedure.

**38.** With back sides together, sew G/H/I unit to left-hand side of two A/B/C/D/E/F units and to right-hand side of two A/B/C/D/E/F units, creating four sections, as shown in block diagram below. Pay close attention to position of units and triangles.

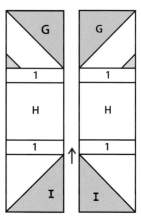

**34.** With back sides together, sew Log Cabin I to bottom of two Blocks G/H and to top of two Blocks G/H, paying attention to light/dark position of Log Cabin I.

**35.** Press seam allowances on front side toward Light Connector 1, and finish seams using the One-Way Street procedure.

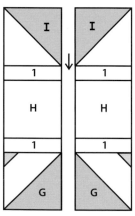

**36.** With back sides together, sew Connector 4 to left side of two G/H/I units and to right-hand side of two G/H/I units, as shown in diagram in next column.

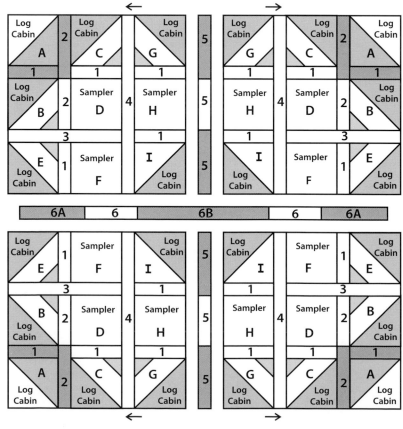

**39.** Press seam allowances on front side toward Connector 4, and finish seams using the One-Way Street procedure.

**40.** With back sides together, sew Connector 5 (dark/light combination) to the four sections, creating two halves. Press, fold and finish each seam with the One-Way Street procedure before proceeding to the next seam.

**41.** With back sides together, sew Connector 6 (dark/light combination) to the two halves, creating one large unit. Press, fold and finish one seam with the One-Way Street procedure before proceeding to the next seam.

## Borders

**1.** Add First, Second and Third Borders in the numerical order listed in the diagram below. Attach borders in the same manner as connectors, using the One-Way Street procedure. Press all seam allowances toward borders before finishing seams.

## Binding

**1.** Trim ⅝" from raw edges of project, leaving a ⅜" seam allowance on all sides.

**2.** Apply French-Fold Binding. (For instructions, see Binding chapter near end of this book.)

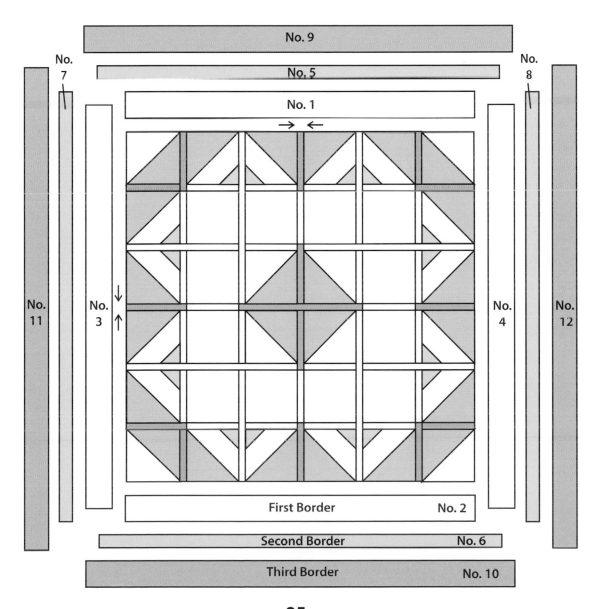

# Bossa Nova Wall Hanging

## (35" x 35")

## Project features:

- Decorative quilting and embroidery
- One-Way Street™ procedure
- Merging Lanes™ procedure on connectors

Reds and greens contrast spectacularly in this Bossa Nova Wall Hanging, which features a combination of quilting techniques. The back side is a solid color that shows off the embroidery and quilting lines. This project also can be used as a table quilt.

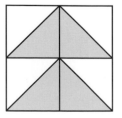
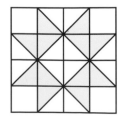

## Basic blocks:

12– 4½" x 4½" Flying Geese Blocks
(5" x 5" unfinished)

4– 9" x 9" Eight-Pointed Star Blocks
(9½" x 9½" unfinished)

## Yardage Requirements

*Based on 42-inch wide fabric*

*See diagram at end of this chapter for placement of pieces.*

### Front Side

**Middle Flying Geese Block (A, B, C, D):**
⅛ yd. each of 4 assorted red prints

**Eight-Pointed Star Block (G, H, I, J):**
⅛ yd. each of 4 assorted green prints

**Corner Flying Geese Block (K, L, M, N):**
⅛ yd. each of 4 assorted brown prints

**Half-Square Triangle E, Background Square F, Anchor Square O, Border P, and Connectors Q, R, S:**
1⅞ yd. beige tone-on-tone

**Connectors T, U, V:** 1⅛ yd. light red

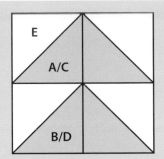
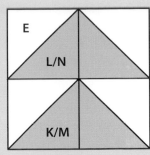

### Back Side

*Back-side pieces are all the same fabric.*

**Flying Geese Blocks, Star Blocks, Anchor Squares, Borders, and Connectors:**
2½ yd. green-gray

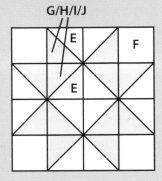

### Binding

⅜ yd. green-gray

### Batting

Cotton Theory Batting, 18" x 2½ yd.

## Fabric Cutting Instructions

Cut carefully to ensure you have an adequate amount of fabric. Cut longest pieces first. Label your cut pieces for each side of the project.

Where strips are listed, cut them on the crosswise grain (selvage to selvage); then cut sub-cuts from each strip on the lengthwise grain. (See diagrams in Preparation chapter for details.)

### Front Side

**Middle Flying Geese Block (A, B, C, D):**
    **From each of 4 assorted red prints:**
    Cut 1– 3⅛" strip
    Sub-cut 4– 3⅛" x 3⅛"

**Eight-Pointed Star Block (G, H, I, J):**
    **From each of 4 assorted green prints:**
    Cut 1– 3⅛" strip
    Sub-cut 6– 3⅛" x 3⅛"

**Corner Flying Geese Block (K, L, M, N):**
    **From each of 4 assorted brown prints:**
    Cut 1– 3⅛" strip
    Sub-cut 2– 3⅛" x 3⅛"

**From beige tone-on-tone:**
    Cut 1– 26" strip
    **Connector S:** Sub-cut 2– 2¾" x 26"
    **Border P:** Sub-cut 8– 8" x 13"
    *(Actual size of this border piece is 6½" x 11". It is cut larger to hoop the quilt layers for machine embroidery.)*

*More fabric cutting instructions on next page*

**From beige tone-on-tone (continued):**
Cut 1– 6½" strip
**Anchor Square O:** Sub-cut 5– 6½" x 6½"
Cut 1– 11" strip
**Connector R:** Sub-cut 4– 2¾" x 11"
**Connector Q:** Sub-cut 10– 2¾" x 6½"
Cut 2– 2¾" strips
**Background Square F:**
Sub-cut 16– 2¾" x 2¾"
Cut 4– 3⅛" strips
**Half-Square Triangle E:**
Sub-cut 48– 3⅛" x 3⅛"

**From light red:**
Cut 1– 36½" strip
**Connector V:** Sub-cut 2– 2¾" x 36½"
**Connector T:** Sub-cut 2– 2¾" x 26"
**Connector U:** Sub-cut 4– 2¾" x 6½"

## Back Side

**From green-gray:**
Cut 2– 11" strips
**Star Blocks:** Sub-cut 4– 11" x 11"
**Middle Flying Geese Blocks:**
Sub-cut 4– 6½" x 11"
Cut 1– 26" strip
**Connector S:**
Sub-cut 2– 2¾" x 26"
**Border P:** Sub-cut 8– 8" x 13"
*(Actual size of this border piece is 6½" x 11". It is cut larger to hoop the quilt layers for machine embroidery.)*
Cut 1– 37" strip
**Connector V:**
Sub-cut
2– 2¾" x 36½"
**Connector T:**
Sub-cut
2– 2¾" x 26"
**Connector R:**
Sub-cut
4– 2¾" x 11"
**Anchor Square O:**
Sub-cut 5– 6½" x 6½"

**Corner Flying Geese Blocks:**
Sub-cut 4– 6½" x 6½"
**Connector Q:** Sub-cut 10– 2¾" x 6½"
**Connector U:** Sub-cut 4– 2¾" x 6½"

## Binding
Cut 4– 2½" x 42" strips

## Batting Cutting Instructions

Cut longest pieces of batting first. Please label your cut pieces.
**Star Block:** Cut 4– 9" x 9"
**Middle Flying Geese Block:** Cut 4– 4½" x 9"
**Corner Flying Geese Block and Anchor Square O:** Cut 9– 4½" x 4½"
**Border P:** Cut 8– 6" x 11"
*(Actual size of Border P batting is 4½" x 9". It is cut larger to hoop the quilt layers for machine embroidery.)*
**Connector Q:** Cut 10– ¾" x 4½"
**Connector R:** Cut 4– ¾" x 9"
**Connector S:** Cut 2– ¾" x 24"
**Connector T:** Cut 2– ¾" x 24"
**Connector U:** Cut 4– ¾" x 4½"
**Connector V:** Cut 2– ¾" x 34½"

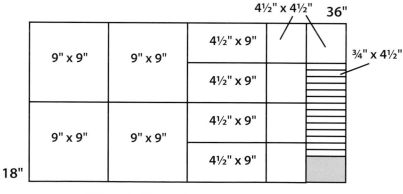

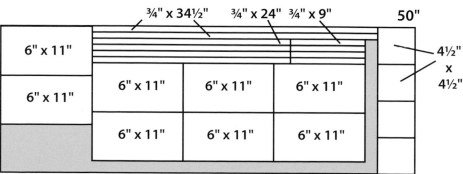

Cutting diagrams for Cotton Theory Batting (18" x 36" and 18" x 50")
*(Gray area denotes batting that is not used)*

**98**

## Piecing Instructions

Insert universal needle size 80/12 into sewing machine.

### Eight-Pointed Star Blocks

*Each block is made up of 12 sets of Half-Square Triangles and four Background Squares.*

1.  Mark a diagonal line on wrong side of Half-Square Triangle E square (beige tone-on-tone 3⅛" x 3⅛").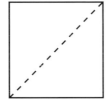

2.  With right sides together, place E on squares G, H, I and J (green prints). You will have six sets for each green print (total of 24 sets).

3.  Sew a ¼" seam on both sides of the diagonal line on E.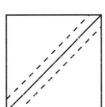

4.  Cut on diagonal line. (This will yield two half-square triangles.)

5.  Press seams open. You will have a total of 48 squares, each made up of two half-square triangles.

Sew 12        Sew 12        Sew 12        Sew 12

6.  Arrange half-square triangles and Background Square F in the order shown in diagrams at top of next column. Use two green prints for each block.

7.  With right sides together, sew pieces into horizontal rows with a ¼" seam.

8.  Press seams open.

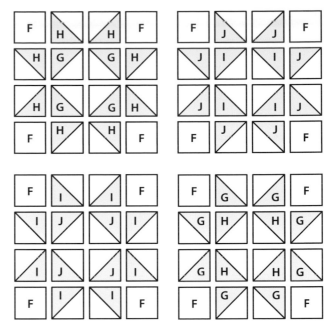

Arrange 4 blocks

9.  Sew rows together with a ¼" seam.

10. Press seams open.

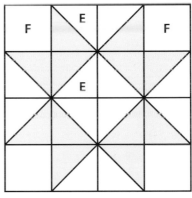

Sew 4 blocks

### Middle Flying Geese Blocks

1.  With right sides together, place E (beige tone-on-tone) on squares A, B, C, and D (red prints). You will have four sets for each red print (total of 16 sets).

2.  Sew a ¼" seam on both sides of the diagonal line on E.

3.  Cut on diagonal line. (This will yield two half-square triangles.)

4.  Press seams open. You will have a total of 32 squares, each made up of two half-square triangles.

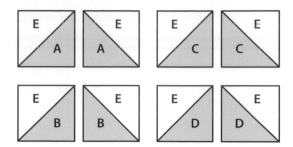

**5.** Arrange pairs as shown in diagram above, using two of the same red print for each pair.

**6.** With right sides together, sew each pair with a ¼" seam.

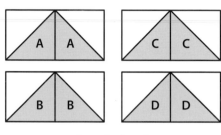

Sew 4 of each

**7.** Press seams open.

**8.** With right sides together and using a ¼" seam, sew A unit to top of B unit and sew C unit to top of D unit to create Flying Geese pairs, as shown in diagram below.

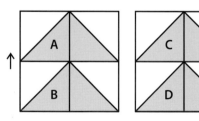

Sew 4 of each

**9.** Press seams toward A unit and C unit.

**10.** With right sides together and using a ¼" seam, sew Flying Geese pairs together.

**11.** Press seam toward B unit.

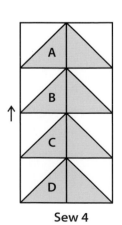

Sew 4

## Corner Flying Geese Blocks

**1.** With right sides together, place square E (beige tone-on-tone) on squares K, L, M, and N (brown prints). You will have two sets for each brown print (total of eight sets).

**2.** Sew a ¼" seam on both sides of the diagonal line on E.

**3.** Cut on diagonal line. (This will yield two half-square triangles.)

**4.** Press seams open. You will have a total of 16 squares, each made up of two half-square triangles.

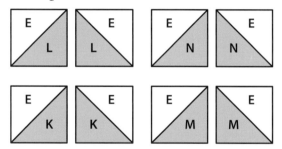

**5.** Arrange pairs as shown in diagram, using two of the same brown print for each pair.

**6.** With right sides together, sew each pair with a ¼" seam.

**7.** Press seams open.

**8.** With right sides together and using a ¼" seam, sew units together, creating Flying Geese pairs, as shown in diagram below.

Sew 2 of each

**9.** Press seams toward L unit and N unit.

Sew 2 of each

# Quilting Instructions

Insert quilting needle size 90/14 into sewing machine. For best results, use a walking foot when quilting layers.

## Eight-Pointed Star Blocks

**Suggested embroidery:** Square feather embroidery design Pfaff 394 Vintage Quilt Blocks, Pattern 7, stitch width 106 mm and length 106 mm. Design available through the Quilt Yard, Osseo, Wisconsin; phone (715) 597-2452 or (800) 673-8075.

**Thread suggestion:** 50-weight dark olive green on top and in bobbin.

**Stitch suggestion:** Zigzag 0.5 mm wide and 3.0 mm long (wobble stitch).

1. Layer fabric and batting. Place back-side Star Block right side down, place batting in center, and place front-side Star Block right side up.

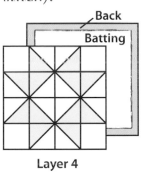

Layer 4

**Note:** Back-side block will be ¾" larger on all four sides than front-side block.

2. Press layers together with steam.

3. Using wobble stitch (0.5 mm wide and 3.0 mm long), quilt in the ditch around star points and center square of Star Block, as shown in red.

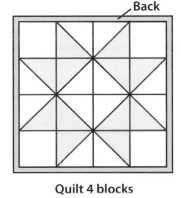

Quilt 4 blocks

4. Place all layers of Star Block in machine embroidery hoop.

5. Size square feather embroidery design to fit center square of Star Block.

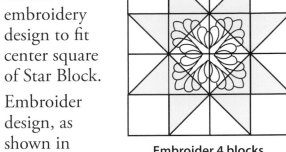

6. Embroider design, as shown in diagram.

Embroider 4 blocks

**Stitch suggestion:** Scallop stitch 9.0 mm wide and 16 mm long.

**Note:** Adding decorative scallop stitches along star point seams will soften the geometric look and camouflage imperfect star points.

7. Using the inside edge of your presser foot, stitch along the four diagonal seam lines shown in diagram, starting at the end away from raw edge. (Scallop stitch should touch the seam line.)

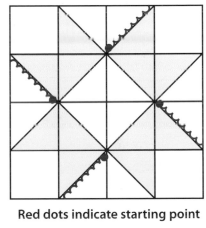

Red dots indicate starting point

8. From the same starting points, sew a mirror image of the scallop stitch along four more diagonal seam lines to complete a "V" design.

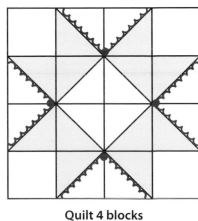

Quilt 4 blocks

## Middle Flying Geese Blocks

1. Layer back-side Middle Flying Geese Block right side down, batting in center, and front-side Middle Flying Geese Block right side up.

**Note:** Back-side block will be ¾" larger on all four sides than front-side block.

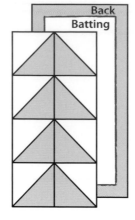

2. Press layers together with steam.

3. Using wobble stitch, quilt in the ditch along triangles, sewing along one side and then the other side, as shown in diagram.

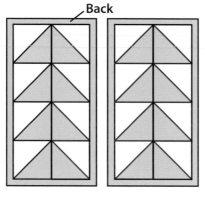

## Corner Flying Geese Blocks

1. Layer back-side Corner Flying Geese Block right side down, batting in center, and front-side Corner Flying Geese Block right side up.

2. Press layers together.

3. Using wobble stitch, quilt in the ditch along triangles, sewing along one side and then other side.

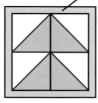

Quilt 4 blocks

## Anchor Square O

1. Mark an X across front of each Anchor Square O.

2. Layer back-side Anchor Square O right side down, batting in center, and front-side Anchor Square O right side up.

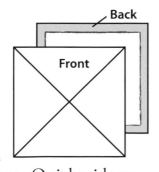

3. Press layers together with steam.

4. Using wobble stitch, quilt on the X, sewing through all layers.

5. Using edge of presser foot as a guide, channel quilt rows across half of the square, alternating directions to compensaate for fabric shifting.

6. Quilt other half of square in same manner.

7. Repeat Steps 5 and 6 following opposite X line to complete a grid, as shown in diagram.

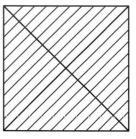

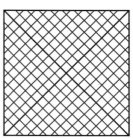

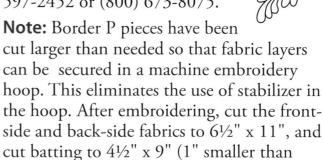

Quilt 5 blocks

## Border P

### Suggested embroidery:

Rectangle feather embroidery design, Anita Goodesigns Quilt Feathers, Pattern 12. Design available through the Quilt Yard, Osseo, Wisconsin; phone (715) 597-2452 or (800) 673-8075.

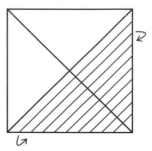

**Note:** Border P pieces have been cut larger than needed so that fabric layers can be secured in a machine embroidery hoop. This eliminates the use of stabilizer in the hoop. After embroidering, cut the front-side and back-side fabrics to 6½" x 11", and cut batting to 4½" x 9" (1" smaller than fabric on all sides).

1. Layer back-side Border P right side down, batting in center, and front-side Border P right side up.

2. Press layers together with steam.

3. Place all layers in machine embroidery hoop.

4. Size feather embroidery design to 106 mm wide and 215 mm long so it fits within a 4" x 8½" area in center of Border P.

5. Embroider design on four Border P blocks.

**Embroider 4**

6. Embroider a mirror image of the design on remaining four Border P blocks.

**Embroider 4**

## Connectors Q, R, S, T, U, V

1. Layer back fabric right side down, batting in center, and front fabric right side up.

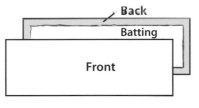

2. Press layers together with steam.

**Thread suggestion:** Match thread to the fabric for each side.

**Stitch suggestion:** Zigzag 0.5 mm wide and 3.0 mm long (wobble stitch).

3. Place Adhesive Quilting Guide 1⅜" to right of sewing machine needle.

4. Quilt down the middle of each connector. (Quilt through entire length.)

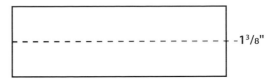

## Assembly Instructions

Insert topstitch needle size 90/14 into sewing machine.

Seam allowances will be finished on front side of this project using the One-Way Street™ procedure, described in Techniques chapter.

**Note:** Use a 1" seam allowance when sewing your quilted pieces together.

**Thread suggestion:** 50-weight barn red cotton on top and 50-weight gray-green cotton in bobbin.

**Stitch suggestion:** Straight stitch 3.5 mm long; joining stitch 6.0 mm wide and 4.0 mm long.

> **Betty's Advice:** *Use the Cotton Theory Adhesive Quilting Guide for accurate seam allowances.*

## Eight-Pointed Star Blocks and Middle Flying Geese Blocks

1. With back sides together (back fabrics against each other) and using a 1" seam, sew Connector R (2¾" x 11") to right-hand side of two Star Blocks, stitching through all layers. (The 1" seam allowance should be at the star points.)

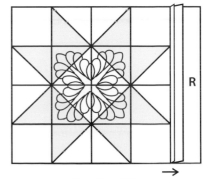

**Construct 2**

**2.** Press the back side; then press all seam allowances on front side toward Connector R.

**3.** Finish seams using the One-Way Street procedure, explained in Techniques chapter. (Trim one layer, fold two.)

**4.** With back sides together, sew two Middle Flying Geese Blocks to Connector R, pointing one Flying Geese Block up and one down, as shown in diagrams below.

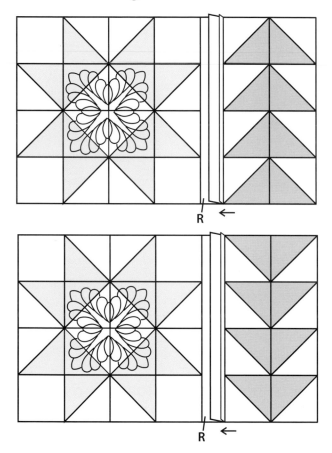

**5.** Press the back side; then press all seam allowances on front side toward Connector R.

**6.** Finish seams using the One-Way Street procedure.

**Note:** Connectors will finish at ¾" wide. After you fold and topstitch the seam allowances, the actual connector will be hidden beneath the folds. The folded edges should touch each other. This is called the Merging Lanes procedure.

**7.** With back sides together, sew Connector R to right-hand side of Middle Flying Geese Blocks, as shown in diagram.

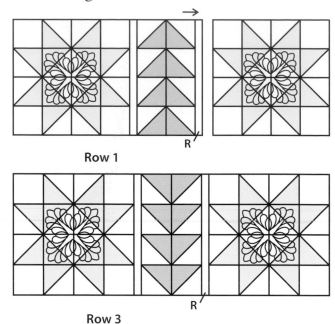

Row 1

Row 3

**8.** Press the back side; then press seam allowances on front side toward Connector R.

**9.** Finish seams using the One-Way Street procedure.

**10.** With back sides together, sew remaining two Star Blocks to Connector R, as indicated in diagram above, to create Rows 1 and 3.

**11.** Press seam allowances on front side toward Connector R.

**12.** Finish seams using the One-Way Street procedure.

## Middle Flying Geese Blocks and Anchor Square O

*All seam allowances will be pressed toward connectors and will be finished using the One-Way Street procedure.*

**1.** With back sides together and using a 1" seam, sew Connector Q to remaining Middle Flying Geese Blocks and to one Anchor Square O, as shown in diagram at right, to create Row 2. Finish each seam using the One-Way Street procedure before continuing to next one.

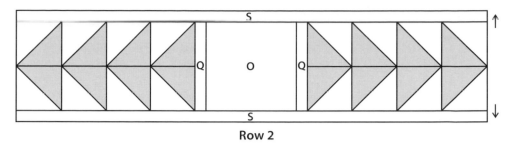

**Row 2**

2. With back sides together, sew Connector S to top and bottom of Row 2 with a 1" seam. Fold and finish seams using the One-Way Street procedure.

3. With back sides together and using a 1" seam, connect Rows 1, 2, and 3. See quilt diagram on next page for placement of rows. Be sure to align intersections, as described in Techniques chapter. Finish seams using the One-Way Street procedure.

## Border P and Anchor Square O

*All seam allowances will be pressed toward connectors and will be finished using the One-Way Street procedure.*

1. With back sides together and using a 1" seam, sew Connector Q to Border P rectangles and Anchor Square O.

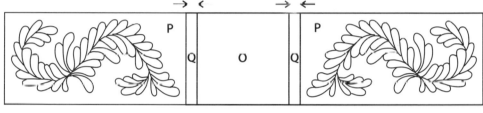

**Construct 4**

Finish each seam using the One-Way Street procedure before continuing to the next one.

2. With back sides together, sew Connector T to bottom of two border units to complete the side borders. Finish seams using the One-Way Street procedure.

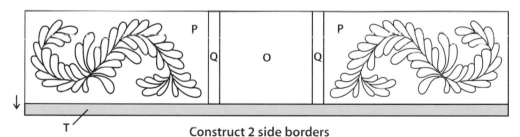

**Construct 2 side borders**

3. With back sides together, sew Connector U and Corner Flying Geese Blocks to ends of two remaining border units to create the top and bottom borders. One set of Flying Geese Blocks should point up and one set should point down, as shown in diagrams. Finish seams using the One-Way Street procedure.

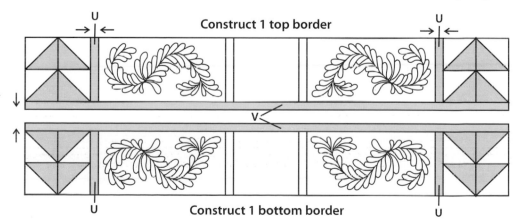

**Construct 1 top border**

**Construct 1 bottom border**

4. With back sides together, sew Connector V to bottom of top border and to top of bottom border, as shown in diagram on previous page. Finish seams using the One-Way Street procedure.

## Attaching Borders

1. With back sides together, sew Connector T to sides of quilt. Finish seams using One-Way Street procedure.

2. With back sides together, sew Connector V to top and bottom of quilt. Finish seams using the One-Way Street procedure.

## Binding

1. Trim ⅝" from raw edges, leaving a ⅜" seam allowance on all sides.

2. Apply French-Fold Binding. (See Binding chapter near end of this book.)

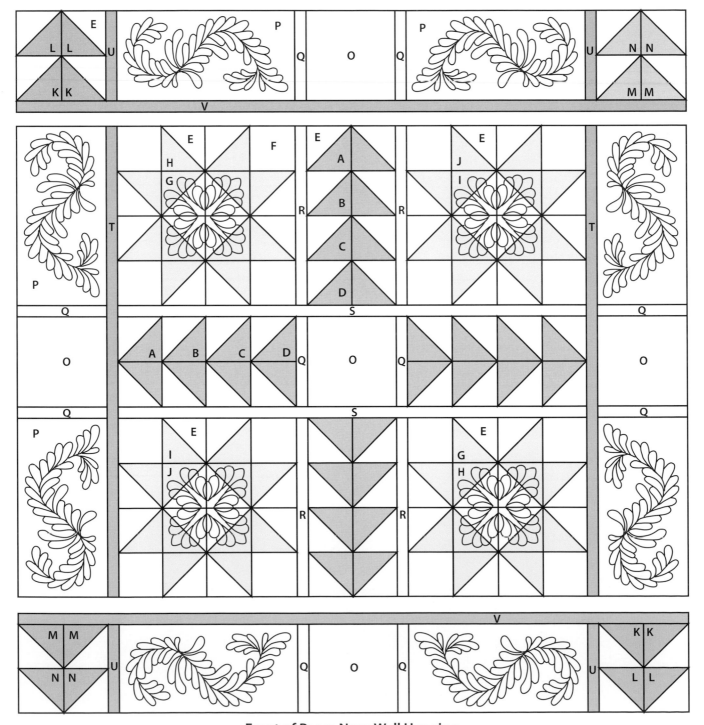

**Front of Bossa Nova Wall Hanging**

# Line Dance Runner

## (24"x 61")

Skill Level
3

**Front and back sides of Line Dance Runner**

## Basic blocks:

11" x 11" Square-in-Square (11½" x 11½" unfinished)
5½" x 11" Square-in-Square (6" x 13" unfinished)

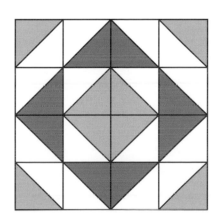

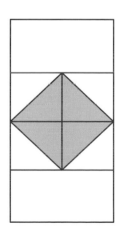

## Project features:

■ Enlarged back-side blocks
■ Bobbin work
■ One-Way Street™ procedure

## Yardage Requirements

*Based on 42-inch wide fabric*

### Front Side

**Square-in-Square Blocks:**

**A:** ¼ yd. first beige print

**B:** ¼ yd. red print

**C:** ¼ yd. second beige print

**D:** ¼ yd. light brown

**E:** ⅛ yd. third beige print

**F:** ⅛ yd. medium brown

**G:** ¼ yd. fourth beige print

**Block Connector:**

**H:** ½ yd. fourth beige print

**Corner Posts:**

**I:** ⅛ yd. fifth beige print

**J:** ⅛ yd. olive green

**Border Connectors:**

**K, L, M:** Total of 1½ yd. dark brown

*This is enough yardage for back side, too.*

**Borders:**

**N, O:** Total of 1½ yd. fourth beige print

### Back Side

**Back of Blocks and Corner Posts:** Total of 1 yd. first beige print

**Block Connector H and Border Connectors K, L, M:** Dark brown fabric left over from front side

**Borders N, O:** Total of 1½ yd. light brown

### Binding

⅜ yd. red/olive green print

### Batting

Cotton Theory Batting, 18" x 2⅞ yd.

## Other Supplies

9– ⅞" off-white buttons (optional)

Three-strand cotton floss in harvest colors

Extra bobbin case for bobbin work

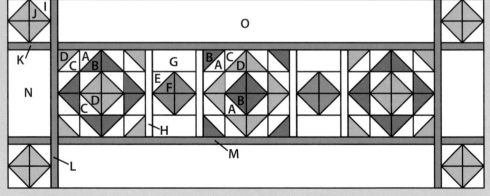

**Front side of Line Dance Runner**

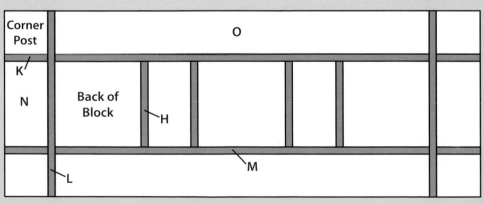

**Back side of Line Dance Runner**

# Fabric Cutting Instructions

Cut carefully to ensure you have an adequate amount of fabric. Label your cut pieces for each side of the project.

Where strips are listed, cut them on the crosswise grain (selvage to selvage); then cut sub-cuts from each strip on the lengthwise grain. (See diagrams in Preparation chapter for details.)

## Front Side

### Square-in-Square Blocks:

**A (first beige print):** Cut 12– 3⅝" x 3⅝"

**B (red print):** Cut 12– 3⅝" x 3⅝"

**C (second beige print):** Cut 12– 3⅝" x 3⅝"

**D (light brown):** Cut 12– 3⅝" x 3⅝"

**E (third beige print):** Cut 4– 3⅝" x 3⅝"

**F (medium brown):** Cut 4– 3⅝" x 3⅝"

**G (fourth beige print):** Cut 4– 6" x 4"

### Block Connector:

**H (fourth beige print):**
Cut 1– 13" strip
Sub-cut 4– 3" x 13"

### Corner Posts:

**I (fifth beige print):** Cut 8– 3⅝" x 3⅝"

**J (olive green):** Cut 8– 3⅝" x 3⅝"

### Border Connectors (dark brown):
*Cut longest pieces first.*
Cut 1– 50" strip
**M:** Sub-cut 2– 3" x 50"
**L:** Sub-cut 2– 3" x 26"
**K:** Sub-cut 4– 3" x 7½"

### Borders (fourth beige print):
*Cut longest pieces first.*
Cut 1– 50" strip
**O:** Sub-cut 2– 7½" x 50"
**N:** Sub-cut 2– 7½" x 13"

## Back Side

### Back of Blocks (first beige print):
Cut 2– 13" strips
Sub-cut 3– 13" x 13"
Sub-cut 2– 7½" x 13"

### Corner Posts (first beige print):
Cut 1– 7½" strip
Sub-cut 4– 7½" x 7½"

### Block Connector and Border Connectors (dark brown yardage from front side):
*Cut longest pieces first.*
Cut 1– 50" strip
**M:** Sub-cut 2– 3" x 50"
**L:** Sub-cut 2– 3" x 26"
**K:** Sub-cut 4– 3" x 7½"
**H:** Sub-cut 4– 3" x 13"

### Borders (light brown):
*Cut longest pieces first.*
Cut 1– 50" strip
**O:** Sub-cut 2– 7½" x 50"
**N:** Sub-cut 2– 7½" x 13"

## Binding

Cut 5– 2½" x 42" strips

# Batting Cutting Instructions

Cut longest pieces of batting first. Please label your cut pieces.

### Blocks:
Cut 3– 11" x 11"
Cut 2– 5½" x 11"

### Corner Posts: Cut 4– 5½" x 5½"

### Block Connector H: Cut 4– 1" x 11"

### Border Connectors:
**K:** Cut 4– 1" x 5½"
**L:** Cut 2– 1" x 24"
**M:** Cut 2– 1" x 48"

### Borders:
**N:** Cut 2– 5½" x 11"
**O:** Cut 2– 5½" x 48"

*See batting cutting diagrams on next page*

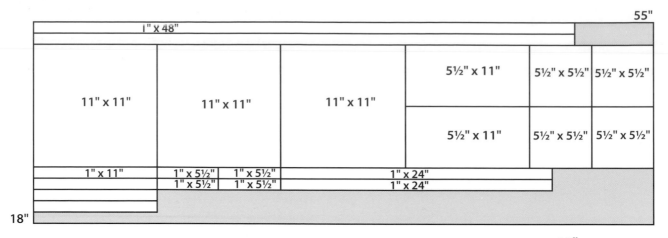

**55"**

| | | | 5½" x 11" | 5½" x 5½" | 5½" x 5½" |
| 11" x 11" | 11" x 11" | 11" x 11" | | | |
| | | | 5½" x 11" | 5½" x 5½" | 5½" x 5½" |

1" x 48"

1" x 11"    1" x 5½"   1" x 5½"    1" x 24"

1" x 5½"   1" x 5½"    1" x 24"

**18"**

**48"**

| 5½" x 48" |
| 5½" x 48" |
| 5½" x 11"    5½" x 11" |

**18"**

**Cutting diagrams for Cotton Theory Batting (18" x 55" and 18" x 48")**
*(Gray area denotes batting that is not used)*

## Piecing Instructions

Insert universal needle size 80/12 into sewing machine.

### Square-in-Square 11" x 11" Block

*This block is made up of 16 sets of half-square triangles.*

1. With right sides together, place square A on square B, and place square C on square D.

2. Mark a diagonal line on wrong side of squares A and C.

3. Sew a ¼" seam on both sides of the diagonal line.

4. Cut on diagonal line. (This will yield two half-square triangles.)

5. Press seam open.

6. Arrange half-square triangles as shown in diagrams below.

Sew 24     Sew 24

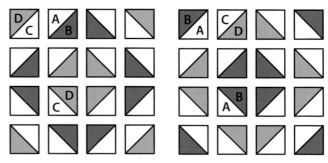

Arrange 2 groups     Arrange 1 group

7. With right sides together, sew half-square triangles together into horizontal rows with a ¼" seam, and then sew rows together.

8. Press seams open.

**110**

## Square-in-Square 5½" x 11" Block

1. With right sides together, place square E on square F.

2. Mark a diagonal line on wrong side of square E.

3. Sew a ¼" seam on both sides of the diagonal line.

4. Cut on diagonal line.

5. Press seam open.

6. Sew four E/F squares together as shown in diagram below.

7. Press seams open.

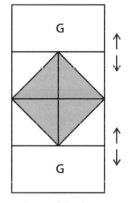

Sew 8

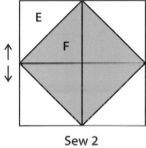

Sew 2

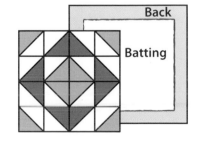

Sew 2 blocks

8. With right sides together, sew rectangle G to top and bottom of E/F units.

9. Press seams open.

## Corner Posts

1. With right sides together, place square I on square J.

2. Mark a diagonal line on wrong side of square I.

3. Sew a ¼" seam on both sides of the diagonal line.

4. Cut on diagonal line.

5. Press seam open.

Sew 16

6. Sew four I/J squares together as shown in diagram.

7. Press seams open.

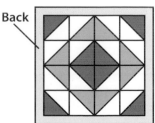

Sew 4 Corner Posts

## Quilting Instructions

Insert quilting needle size 90/14 into sewing machine. For best results, use a walking foot when quilting layers.

**Note:** Cotton floss is used in the bobbin for most of the quilting in this project. Bobbin work using floss, ribbon, or yarn makes the quilting more pronounced. (See Techniques chapter for details.)

**Stitch suggestion:** Zigzag stitch 0.5 mm wide and 3.0 mm long (wobble stitch).

**Thread suggestion:** 40-weight brown variegated cotton thread on top and three-strand variegated cotton floss in harvest colors in bobbin.

> **Betty's Advice:** Loosen or bypass the bobbin tension when using floss in your bobbin.

## Square-in-Square 11" x 11" Block

1. Layer fabric and batting. With back fabric right side down, place batting in center, and place Square-in-Square block right side up.

**Note:** Back-side fabric will be ¾" larger than front-side block on all sides.

**2.** Press layers together with steam.

**3.** Quilt in the ditch using wobble stitch, as shown in diagram.

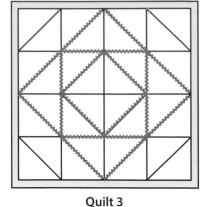

Quilt 3

**Thread change:**
40-weight beige cotton thread on top and 50-weight beige cotton thread in bobbin.

**4.** Quilt in the ditch on seam of outside corner triangles, as shown in diagram.

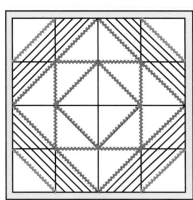

Quilt 3

**5.** Using edge of presser foot as a guide, quilt four additional rows, as indicated in diagram.

**Note:** Because widths of presser feet vary, the number of rows of quilting may vary.

**Helpful hint:** Measure quilted block from raw edge to raw edge of back-side fabric after quilting. Border N will need to be the same length as this after quilting.

## Square-in-Square 5½" x 11" Block

**Thread change:** 40-weight brown variegated cotton thread on top and three-strand variegated cotton floss in harvest colors in bobbin.

**1.** Layer back fabric right side down, batting in center, and rectangular Square-in-Square Block right side up.

**Note:** Back-side fabric will be ¾" larger than front-side block on two long sides. Top and bottom of front-side block will be even with back-side fabric.

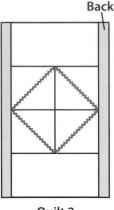

Back

**2.** Press layers together with steam.

**3.** Quilt in the ditch using wobble stitch, as shown in diagram.

Quilt 2

**Thread change:** 40-weight beige cotton thread on top and 50-weight beige cotton thread in bobbin.

**4.** Using edge of presser foot as a guide, quilt five additional rows, as shown in diagram.

## Corner Posts

**Thread change:** 40-weight brown variegated cotton thread on top and three-strand variegated cotton floss in harvest colors in bobbin.

Quilt 2

**1.** Layer back fabric right side down, batting in center, and front-side Corner Post right side up.

**2.** Press layers together with steam.

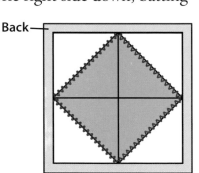

Back

**3.** Quilt in the ditch using wobble stitch.

Quilt 4

## Block Connector H

**Thread change:** 40-weight beige cotton thread on top and 50-weight beige cotton thread in bobbin.

**1.** Layer back fabric right side down, batting in center, and front fabric right side up.

2. Press layers together with steam.

3. Place Adhesive Quilting Guide 1⅜" to right of sewing machine needle to provide a straight quilting row.

4. Quilt down each side of Block Connector H, 1⅜" from raw edge. (Quilt through the entire length.)

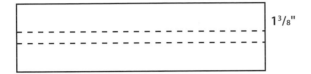
1³/₈"

## Border Connectors K, L, M

**Thread change:** Match thread to fabric for each side.

1. Layer back fabric right side down, batting in center, and front fabric right side up.

2. Press layers together with steam.

3. Quilt in same manner as Block Connector H.

## Borders N, O

**Note:** Bobbin work is used on the front and back of the borders to create texture, color, and a directional design.

**Thread change:** 40-weight brown variegated cotton thread on top and three-strand variegated cotton floss in harvest colors in bobbin.

*Betty's Advice:*
*To camouflage imperfect tension when doing bobbin work, match the color of the top thread to the bobbin floss.*

1. Layer back fabric right side down, batting in center, and front fabric right side up.

2. Press layers together with steam.

3. Place Adhesive Quilting Guide 3¾" to the right of sewing machine needle.

4. With back side facing up, quilt down the middle of Borders N and O using a wobble stitch.

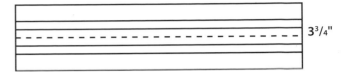
3³/₄"

5. Place Adhesive Quilting Guide 2¾" to the right of sewing machine needle.

6. Quilt 1" away on both sides of previous quilting.

7. Place Adhesive Quilting Guide 1¾" to the right of sewing machine needle.

8. Quilt 1" away from previous quilting (total of five rows).

9. Turn borders over, with front side facing up.

**Thread change:** 40-weight beige cotton thread on top and beige/tan lightweight yarn in bobbin.

10. Quilt between the previously quilted rows (four more rows).

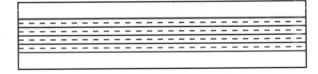

**Note:** Border N should be same length as quilted Square-in-Square Block, measuring from raw edge to raw edge of back-side fabric. If it is not, trim Border N to correct length.

## Assembly Instructions

Insert topstitch needle size 90/14 into sewing machine.

Seam allowances will be finished on front side of this project using the One-Way Street™ procedure, described in Techniques chapter.

**Note:** Use a 1" seam allowance when sewing your quilted pieces together.

**Thread suggestion:**
40-weight brown variegated cotton on top and in bobbin.

**Stitch suggestion:**
Straight stitch 3.5 mm long; joining stitch 6.0 mm wide and 4.0 mm long.

## Blocks and Block Connectors

1. Arrange blocks as shown in finished diagram on next page.

2. With back sides together (back fabrics against each other) and using a 1" seam, sew Block Connector H to both sides of Square-in-Square 5½" x 11" Blocks. Stitch through all layers.

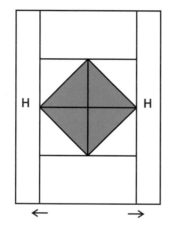

3. Press the back side; then press all seam allowances on front side toward Block Connector H.

4. Finish seams using the One-Way Street procedure, explained in Techniques chapter. (Trim one layer, fold two.)

5. With back sides together and using a 1" seam, sew these units to Square-in-Square 11" x 11" Blocks, as shown in diagram.

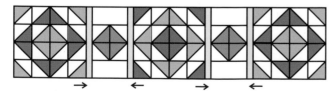

6. Press seam allowances on front side toward Block Connector H.

7. Finish seams using the One-Way Street procedure.

## Border Connector M and Border O

*Border connectors will be sewn to borders and then attached to runner.*

1. With back sides together, sew Border Connector M to long sides of Border O with a 1" seam.

2. Press seam allowances on front side toward Border Connector M.

3. Finish seams using the One-Way Street procedure.

4. With back sides together and using a 1" seam, sew Border O units to runner, as shown in diagram.

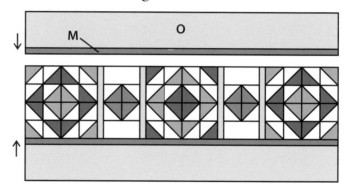

5. Press seam allowances on front side toward Border Connector M.

6. Finish seams using the One-Way Street procedure.

## Corner Posts and Border Connector K

1. With back sides together, sew Border Connector K to Corner Posts with a 1" seam.

2. Press seam allowances on front side toward Border Connector K.

Construct 4

3. Finish seams using the One-Way Street procedure.

## Border N

1. With back sides together and using a 1" seam, sew Border N to Corner Post units, as shown in diagram.

2. Press seam allowances on front side toward Border Connector K.

3. Finish seams using the One-Way Street procedure.

## Border Connector L

1. With back sides together and using a 1" seam, sew Border Connector L to one side of Border N units, as shown in diagram.

2. Press seam allowances on front side toward Border Connector L.

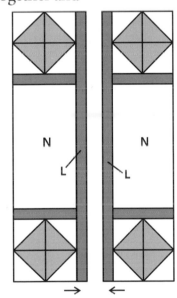

**Construct 2**

3. Finish seams using the One-Way Street procedure.

4. With back sides together and using a 1" seam, sew side borders to runner, as shown in diagram at bottom of page. Be sure to align intersections, as described in Techniques chapter.

5. Press seam allowances on front side toward Border Connector L.

6. Finish seams using the One-Way Street procedure.

## Adding Buttons (optional)

1. Sew ⅞" buttons to center of each Corner Post and Square-in-Square Block.

## Binding

1. Trim ⅝" from raw edges of project, leaving a ⅜" seam allowance on all sides.

2. Apply French-Fold Binding. (For instructions, see Binding chapter near end of this book.)

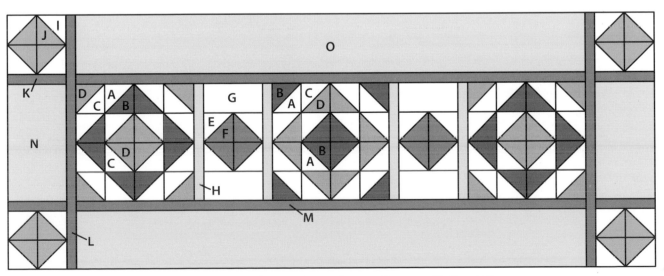

**Front side of finished Line Dance Runner (24" x 61")**

# American Promenade Quilt

### (94" x 94")

Log Cabin Blocks are arranged to create a diamond design in this scrappy, reversible Cotton Theory quilt. The front side is shown here, and the back side is on the next page, along with instructions.

## Project features:

- Enlarged back-side blocks
- Bobbin work
- One-Way Street™ procedure
- Reversible binding

**Back side of American Promenade Quilt**

**Basic blocks:** 36– 12" x 12" Log Cabin Blocks (12½" x 12½" unfinished)

36– 12" x 12" Half-Square Triangle Blocks (14" x 14" unfinished)

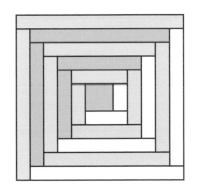

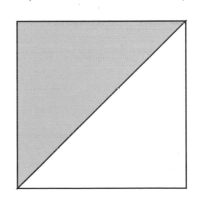

## Yardage Requirements

*Based on 42-inch wide fabric*

### Front Side

*The photo of the front side of this quilt shows Log Cabin Blocks that are scrappy, with a mixture of prints and colors. Yardage listed below is the total needed for light and dark fabrics. If you want a scrappy look, divide each yardage total accordingly.*

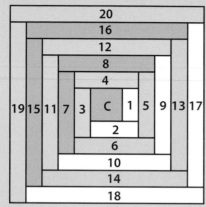

### Log Cabin Blocks:

**Center (C):** ¼ yd. first dark red

**Logs 1, 2, 9, 10, 17, 18:**
2 yd. first light cream or beige

**Logs 3, 4, 11, 12, 19, 20:** 2¼ yd. second dark red or dark blue

**Logs 5, 6, 13, 14:** 1⅜ yd. second light cream or beige

**Logs 7, 8, 15, 16:** 1½ yd. third dark red or dark blue

*See diagram at end of this chapter for placement of Connectors and Borders.*

**Connectors A and B:**
1⅝ yd. second light cream or beige

**Connectors C and D:**
⅞ yd. third dark red or dark blue

**First Border:** 1⅛ yd. first dark red

**Second Border:**
2¾ yd. first light cream or beige

### Back Side

**Half-Square Triangle Blocks:**
18 assorted light cream or beige fat quarters
18 assorted dark gold or rust fat quarters

**Connectors A and B:**
1⅝ yd. light cream or beige

**Connectors C and D:** ⅞ yd. dark gold or rust

**First Border:** 1⅛ yd. dark brown

**Second Border:** 2¾ yd. light cream or beige

### Reversible Binding

**Front side:** ¾ yd. dark red or dark blue
**Back side:** ⅜ yd. dark gold or rust

### Batting

Cotton Theory Batting, 18" x 17 yd.

## Fabric Cutting Instructions

Cut carefully to ensure you have an adequate amount of fabric. Label your cut pieces for each side of the project.

Where strips are listed, cut them on the crosswise grain (selvage to selvage); then cut sub-cuts from each strip on the lengthwise grain. (See diagrams in Preparation chapter for details.)

### Front Side

**Log Cabin Blocks:**

**Center (first dark red):**
Cut 3– 2½" strips
Sub-cut 36– 2½" x 2½"

**Logs 1 and 2 (first light cream or beige):**
Cut 3– 3½" strips
**Log 2:** Sub-cut 36– 1½" x 3½"
**Log 1:** Sub-cut 36– 1½" x 2½"

*More fabric cutting instructions on next page*

**Logs 3 and 4 (second dark red or blue):**
Cut 3– 4½" strips
**Log 4:** Sub-cut 36– 1½" x 4½"
**Log 3:** Sub-cut 36– 1½" x 3½"

**Logs 5 and 6 (second cream or beige):**
Cut 3– 5½" strips
**Log 6:** Sub-cut 36– 1½" x 5½"
**Log 5:** Sub-cut 36– 1½" x 4½"

**Logs 7 and 8 (third dark red or blue):**
Cut 3– 6½" strips
**Log 8:** Sub-cut 36– 1½" x 6½"
**Log 7:** Sub-cut 36– 1½" x 5½"

**Logs 9 and 10 (first cream or beige):**
Cut 3– 7½" strips
**Log 10:** Sub-cut 36– 1½" x 7½"
**Log 9:** Sub-cut 36– 1½" x 6½"

**Logs 11 and 12
(second dark red or blue):**
Cut 3– 8½" strips
**Log 12:** Sub-cut 36– 1½" x 8½"
**Log 11:** Sub-cut 36– 1½" x 7½"

**Logs 13 and 14 (second cream or beige):**
Cut 3– 9½" strips
**Log 14:** Sub-cut 36– 1½" x 9½"
**Log 13:** Sub-cut 36– 1½" x 8½"

**Logs 15 and 16 (third dark red or blue):**
Cut 3– 10½" strips
**Log 16:** Sub-cut 36– 1½" x 10½"
**Log 15:** Sub-cut 36– 1½" x 9½"

**Logs 17 and 18 (first cream or beige):**
Cut 3  11½" strips
**Log 18:** Sub-cut 36– 1½" x 11½"
**Log 17:** Sub-cut 36– 1½" x 10½"

**Logs 19 and 20 (first dark red or blue):**
Cut 3– 12½" strips
**Log 20:** Sub-cut 36– 1½" x 12½"
**Log 19:** Sub-cut 36– 1½" x 11½"

**Connector A (second cream or beige):**
Cut 2– 14" strips
Sub-cut 18– 3" x 14"

**Connector B (second cream or beige):**
Cut 1– 27" strip
Sub-cut 9– 3" x 27"

**Connector C (third dark red or blue):**
Cut 1– 27" strip
Sub-cut 6– 3" x 27"

**Connector D (third dark red or blue):**
Use leftover yardage from Connector C
Sub-cut 6– 3" x 27"
Piece together short ends of sub-cuts
Sub-cut 2– 3" x 79"

**First Border (first dark red):**
Cut 1– 36" strip
Sub-cut 10– 4" x 36"
Piece together short ends of sub-cuts
Sub-cut 2– 4" x 83"
Sub-cut 2– 4" x 79"

**Second Border (first light cream or beige):**
Cut 1– 95" strip
Sub-cut 2– 8" x 95"
Sub-cut 2– 8" x 83"

## Back Side

**Half-Square Triangle Blocks:**
   **From each of 18 light fat quarters:**
   Cut 1– 14½" x 14½" (total of 18)
   **From each of 18 dark fat quarters:**
   Cut 1– 14½" x 14½" (total of 18)

**Connector A (light cream or beige):**
Cut 2– 14" strips
Sub-cut 18– 3" x 14"

**Connector B (light cream or beige):**
Cut 1– 27" strip
Sub-cut 9– 3" x 27"

**Connector C (dark gold or rust):**
Cut 1– 27" strip
Sub-cut 6– 3" x 27"

**Connector D (dark gold or rust):**
Use leftover yardage from Connector C
Sub-cut 6– 3" x 27"
Piece together short ends of sub-cuts
Sub-cut 2– 3" x 79"

*More fabric cutting instructions on next page*

**First Border (dark brown):**
Cut 1– 36" strip
Sub-cut 10– 4" x 36"
Piece together short ends of sub-cuts
Sub-cut 2– 4" x 83"
Sub-cut 2– 4" x 79"

**Second Border (light cream or beige):**
Cut 1– 95" strip
Sub-cut 2– 8" x 95"
Sub-cut 2– 8" x 83"

## Reversible Binding
**Front side (dark red or dark blue):**
Cut 10– 2¼"x 42" strips
**Back side (dark gold or rust):**
Cut 10– 1¼"x 42" strips

## Batting Cutting Instructions
Cut longest pieces of batting first. Please label your cut pieces.
**Blocks:** Cut 36– 12" x 12"
**Connector A:** Cut 18– 1" x 12"
**Connector B:** Cut 9– 1" x 25"
**Connector C:** Cut 6– 1" x 25"
**Connector D:** Cut 2– 1" x 77"
**First Border:**
Cut 2– 2" x 81"
Cut 2– 2" x 77"
**Second Border:**
Cut 2– 6" x 93"
Cut 2– 6" x 81"

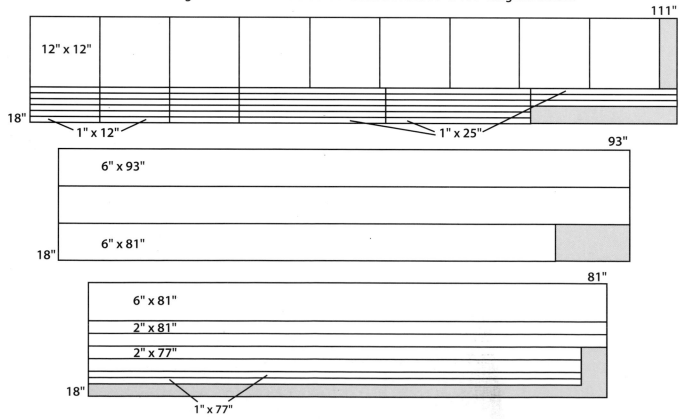

Cut three of these, so you have a total of 27 blocks measuring 12" x 12".
The remaining nine 12" x 12" blocks are included in the 18" x 111" diagram below.

**Cutting diagrams for Cotton Theory Batting (18" x 111", 18" x 108", 18" x 93", and 18" x 81")**
*(Gray area denotes batting that is not used)*

## Piecing Instructions

Insert universal needle size 80/12 into sewing machine.

### Log Cabin Blocks (Front Side)

1. With right sides together and using a ¼" seam, sew Log 1 to right-hand side of Center.

2. Press seam allowances toward Log 1.

3. With right sides together and using a ¼" seam, sew Log 2 to bottom of Center unit, and press seam allowances toward Log 2.

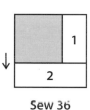

4. With right sides together, sew Log 3 to left side of Center unit, and press seam allowances toward Log 3.

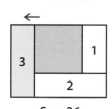

5. With right sides together, sew Log 4 to top of Center unit, and press seam allowances toward Log 4.

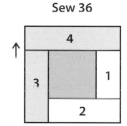

6. Continue adding Logs 5 through 20 clockwise to complete Log Cabin Block, pressing after sewing each seam.

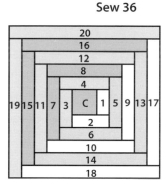

### Half-Square Triangle Blocks (Back Side)

1. With right sides together, place one light 14½" square on one dark 14½" square.

2. Mark a diagonal line on wrong side of light square.

3. Sew a ¼" seam on both sides of diagonal line.

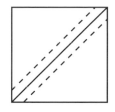
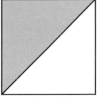

Sew 36

4. Cut on diagonal line. (This will yield two half-square triangles.)

5. Press seam open.

## Quilting Instructions

Insert quilting needle size 90/14 into sewing machine. For best results, use a walking foot when quilting layers.

### Log Cabin and Half-Square Triangle Blocks:

1. Layer fabric and batting. Place Half-Square Triangle Block right side down, place batting in center, and place Log Cabin Block right side up, keeping dark sections and light sections of blocks together.

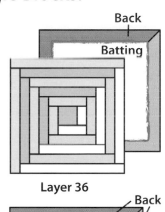

**Note:** Back-side Half-Square Triangle Block will be ¾" larger than the front-side Log Cabin Block on all sides.

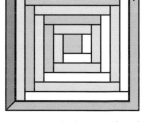

2. Press layers together with steam.

3. Pin layers to secure them during quilting.

4. Turn pressed layers over so that Half-Square Triangle Block is facing up.

**Stitch suggestion:** Zigzag 0.5 mm wide and 3.0 mm long (wobble stitch).

**Thread suggestion:** 40-weight variegated gold/rust cotton on top and 40-weight variegated navy cotton in bobbin.

5. Using wobble stitch, quilt in the ditch of Half-Square Triangle seam.

6. Mark 1" diagonal intervals on dark portion of block.

7. Quilt 1" from previous quilting.

8. Continue adding quilting rows 1" apart, alternating directions to compensate for fabric shifting.

9. Turn block over so that front-side Log Cabin Block is facing up.

**Stitch suggestion:** Light and airy zigzag or decorative stitch of your choice.

**Thread suggestion:** Switch top and bobbin threads. Use 40-weight variegated navy cotton on top and 40-weight variegated gold/rust cotton in bobbin.

10. Quilt in the ditch on light portion of Log Cabin Block, forming an L shape for every round.

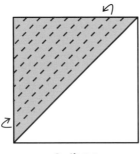

Quilt 36

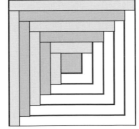

Red lines indicate decorative stitching

*Betty's Advice:* Using a wobble stitch when quilting in the ditch will create an illusion of movement in your blocks.

11. Trim back-side Half-Square Triangle Block to 14" x 14", if necessary. (Front-side block will remain smaller than back-side block.)

## Connectors A, B, C, and D

1. Pair up back-side and front-side Connectors A, B, C, and D.

2. Layer back fabric right side down, batting in center, and front fabric right side up.

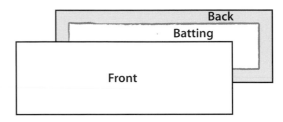

3. Press layers together with steam.

4. Place Adhesive Quilting Guide 1⅜" to right of sewing machine needle.

5. Using wobble stitch (zigzag 0.5 mm wide and 3.0 mm long), quilt down both long sides of each connector (total of two rows). (Quilt through entire length of connectors.)

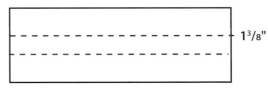

1⅜"

Quilt 18  Connector A
Quilt 9 Connector B
Quilt 6 Connector C
Quilt 2 Connector D

## First Border

1. Layer back fabric right side down, batting in center, and front fabric right side up.

2. Press layers together with steam.

3. Pin layers to secure them during quilting.

4. Using wobble stitch, quilt down both long sides 1⅜" from raw edges.

**5.** Using edge of presser foot as a guide along previously quilted rows, quilt one more row toward the middle of the border, as shown in diagram (total of four rows).

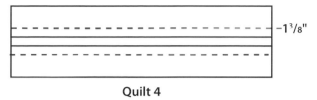

**Quilt 4**

## Second Border

**Note:** Bobbin work featuring a fingering-weight yarn was used on this border instead of thread to give the quilting a heavier look.

**Thread suggestion:** 40-weight variegated brown cotton on top and Anazazi fingering-weight variegated alpaca yarn in bobbin. (If you prefer, you can use the same thread in bobbin as on top, instead of yarn.)

**1.** Layer back fabric right side down, batting in center, and front fabric right side up.

**2.** Press layers, and pin them together.

**3.** Mark an X on one end of each Second Border piece, as shown in diagram. (To do this, fold the bottom and top corners up and down, setting two crease lines at a 45-degree angle.)

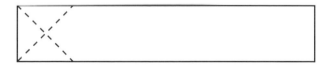

**4.** Using wobble stitch (zigzag 0.5 mm wide and 3.0 mm long), quilt on one of the crease lines, stopping ¾" to ⅞" from raw edge on long side of border. Pivot, travel along seam allowance, and

Pivot

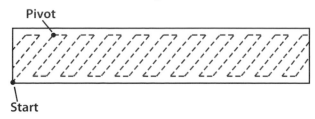

Start

quilt 1" intervals across entire border, as shown in diagram at bottom of previous column. (Do not quilt within ¾" of raw edges on long sides.)

**5.** Quilt upper left triangular space in same manner, as shown in diagram in previous column.

**6.** Quilt on the other crease line, and repeat diagonal quilting in opposite direction across the entire border.

Start

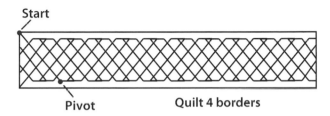

Pivot          **Quilt 4 borders**

## Assembly Instructions

Insert topstitch needle size 90/14 into sewing machine.

Seam allowances will be finished on both sides of this project using the One-Way Street™ procedure, described in Techniques chapter.

**Note:** Use a 1" seam allowance when sewing your quilted pieces together.

**Thread suggestion:**
40-weight variegated navy cotton on top and 40-weight variegated gold/rust cotton in bobbin.

**Stitch suggestion:**
Straight stitch 3.5 mm long; joining stitch 6.0 mm wide and 4.0 mm long.

*Betty's Advice: Use the Cotton Theory Adhesive Quilting Guide for accurate 1" seams.*

## Connector A

1. Arrange Log Cabin Blocks into groups of four, with light sections toward the middle, as shown in diagram.

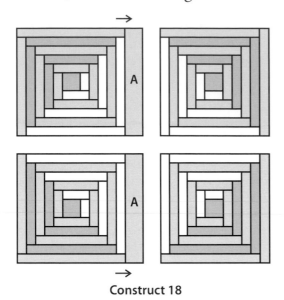

**Construct 18**

2. With back sides together (back fabrics against each other) and using a 1" seam, sew Connector A (3" x 14") to right-hand side of two Log Cabin Blocks, as indicated in diagram. Sew through all layers.

3. Press the back side; then press all seam allowances on front side toward Connector A.

4. Finish seams using the One-Way Street procedure, explained in Techniques chapter. (Trim one layer, fold two.)

5. Repeat Steps 2 through 4 for remaining groups of four Log Cabin Blocks.

6. With back sides together and using a 1" seam, sew other long edge of Connector A to left-hand side of two remaining Log Cabin Blocks in each group.

7. Press the back side; then press all seam allowances on front side toward Connector A.

8. Finish seams using the One-Way Street procedure.

## Connector B

1. With back sides together and using a 1" seam, sew Connector B (3" x 27") to bottom of nine Log Cabin/Connector A units, paying close attention to position of light sections of Log Cabin Blocks, as shown in diagram.

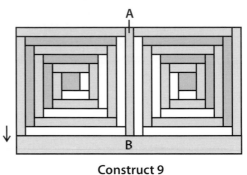

**Construct 9**

2. Press the back side; then press all seam allowances on front side toward Connector B.

3. Finish seams using the One-Way Street procedure.

4. Align intersections of top and bottom units in each Log Cabin group, as described in Techniques chapter.

5. With back sides together, sew bottom unit to top unit, creating a diamond design, as shown in diagram.

**Construct 9 diamond units**

6. Press seam allowances on front side toward Connector B, and finish seams using the One-Way Street procedure.

## Connector C

**Note:** Seam allowances will be finished on back side of quilt, instead of front side.

1. With front sides together and using a 1" seam, sew Connector C to right-hand side of six diamond units.

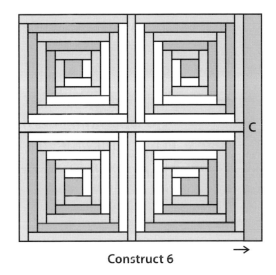

Construct 6

2. Press front side; then press seam allowances on back side toward Connector C.

3. Finish seams using the One Way Street procedure.

4. Arrange diamond units into horizontal rows, as shown in diagram on next page, and align intersections (described in Techniques chapter).

5. With front sides together, sew three diamond units together in each horizontal row, finishing each seam before connecting another unit.

6. Press seam allowances on back side toward Connector C.

7. Finish seams using the One-Way Street procedure.

## Connector D

1. With front sides together and using a 1" seam, sew Connector D to bottom of two rows.

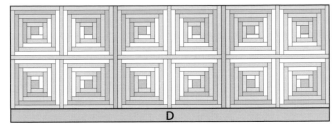

Construct 2

2. Press seam allowances on back side toward Connector D.

3. Finish seams using the One-Way Street procedure.

4. Align intersections between rows.

5. With front sides together, connect the three rows.

6. Press seam allowances on back side toward Connector D.

7. Finish seams using the One-Way Street procedure.

## First and Second Borders

**Note:** Seam allowances will be finished on front side of quilt. Fold and topstitch each border seam before adding additional borders.

1. With back sides together and using a 1" seam, sew First Border to top and bottom of quilt, and then to the sides, pressing all seam allowances toward First Border and finishing each seam with the One-Way Street procedure. See diagram on next page for placement of borders.

2. With back sides together, sew Second Border to top and bottom of quilt, and then to the sides, pressing all seam allowances toward Second Border and finishing each seam with the One-Way Street procedure.

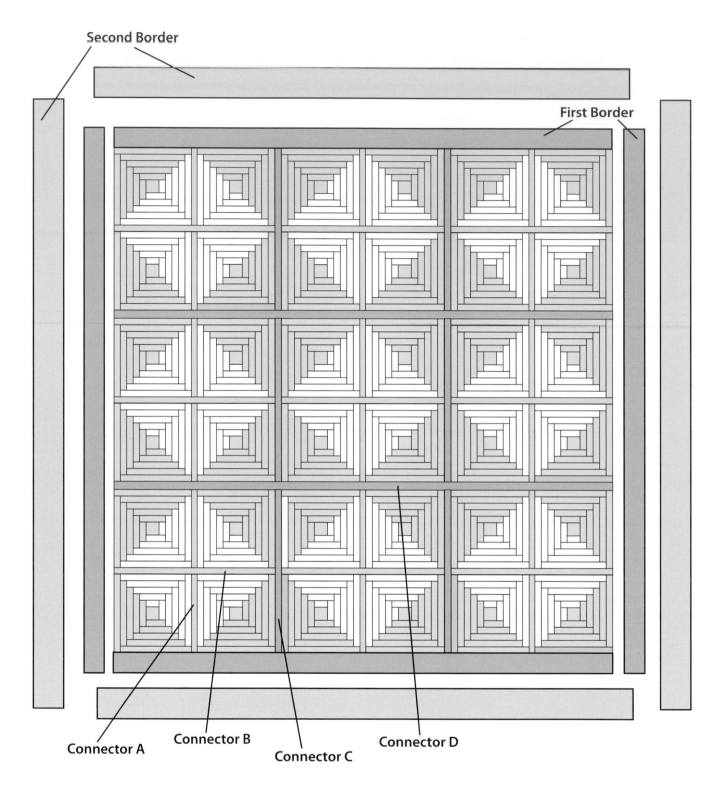

**Front of American Promenade Quilt**

## Binding

1. Trim ½" from raw edges of quilt, leaving a ½" seam allowance on all sides.
2. Apply Reversible Binding. (For instructions, see Binding chapter near end of this book.)

# Tulip Tango Placemats

## Set of Four Placemats (13"x 17" each)
## and Napkins (15½" x 15½" each)

**Tulip Tango Placemat with folded napkin**

## Project features:
- One-Way Street™ procedure
- Bias Binding
- Napkins with mitered corners

**Basic block:** 8" x 8" Four-Patch
Variation (8½" x 8½" unfinished)

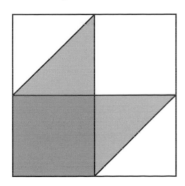

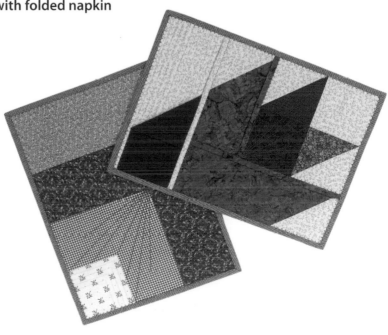

**Front and back sides of Tulip Tango Placemat**

## Yardage Requirements

*Based on 42-inch wide fabric*

*This yardage is enough for four placemats.*

### Front Side

**Flower C, D:** ¼ yd. each of 3 assorted red prints

**Background A, B, E, H:** ¾ yd. beige print

**Leaves F, G:** ¾ yd. dark olive green

**Pocket P:** 1 fat eighth dark olive green wool

**Napkins N (optional):**
1 yd. green/beige/red print

### Back Side

**Back of Block A:** 1 fat quarter beige print

**Back of Block BC, BCD:** 1 fat quarter red check

**Back of Leaves F, G:** ¾ yd. red print

**Extension H:** ½ yd. red/beige print

### Bias Binding

⅝ yd. green/beige check

### Batting

Cotton Theory Batting, 18" x 48"

## Fabric Cutting Instructions

Cut carefully to ensure you have an adequate amount of fabric. Label your cut pieces for each side. Where strips are listed, cut them on the crosswise grain (selvage to selvage); then cut sub-cuts from each strip on the lengthwise grain. (See diagrams in Preparation chapter for details.)

### Front Side

#### For Four-Patch Variation Block

 **A (beige print):** Cut 4– 4½" x 4½"

 **B (beige print):** Cut 4– 4⅞" x 4⅞"

 **C (first red print):** Cut 2– 4⅞" x 4⅞"

 **C (second red print):** Cut 2– 4⅞" x 4⅞"

 **D (third red print):** Cut 4– 4½" x 4½"

**E (beige print):** Cut 8– 6" x 6"

**F (dark olive green):**
Cut 1– 10" strip
Sub-cut 4– 6" x 10"

**G (dark olive green):**
Cut 1– 14" strip
Sub-cut 4– 6" x 14"

**H (beige print):**
Cut 1– 14" strip
Sub-cut 4– 6" x 14"

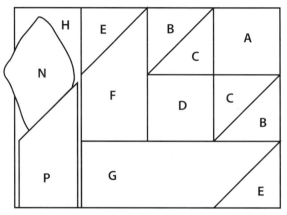

**Front side of Tulip Tango Placemat (set of four)**
*Two placemats will be mirror images of the others.*

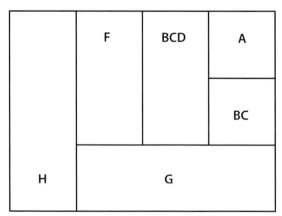

**Back side of Tulip Tango Placemat (set of four)**
*Two placemats will be mirror images of the others.*

**P (dark olive green wool):**
Cut 4– 4" x 8"

**N (green/beige/red print):**
Cut 4– 18" x 18"

## Back Side

**A (beige print):** Cut 4– 5¼" x 5¼"

**BC (red check):** Cut 4– 5¼" x 5¼"

**BCD (red check):** Cut 4– 5¼" x 10"

**F (red print):**
Cut 1– 10" strip
Sub-cut 4– 6" x 10"

**G (red print):**
Cut 1– 14" strip
Sub-cut 4– 6" x 14"

**H (red/beige print):**
Cut 1– 14" strip
Sub-cut 4– 6" x 14"

## Bias Binding

Cut 2– 21" x 21" squares

Cut squares into 2½" bias strips by following instructions in Binding chapter near end of this book.

## Batting Cutting Instructions

Please label your cut pieces.

**Block:** Cut 4– 8" x 8"

**Leaves (F):** Cut 4– 4" x 8"

**Leaves (G):** Cut 4– 4" x 12"

**Extension (H):**
Cut 4 5" x 12"

Cutting diagram for Cotton Theory Batting (18" x 48")

*(Gray area denotes batting that is not used)*

## Piecing Instructions

Insert universal needle size 80/12 into sewing machine.

### Four-Patch Variation Block

1. With right sides together, place square B on square C so one square covers the other.

2. Mark a diagonal line on wrong side of square B.

3. Sew a ¼" seam on both sides of the diagonal line.

4. Cut on diagonal line. (This will yield two half-square triangles.)

Sew 2 using each C red print (total of 4)

5. Press seam open.

6. With right sides together, sew half-square triangles BC to front-side square A with a ¼" seam, as shown in diagram.

7. Press seam open.

8. With right sides together, sew other half-square triangles BC to square D with a ¼" seam.

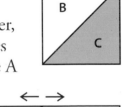

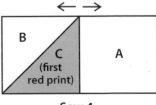

Sew 4

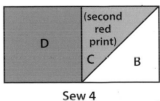

Sew 4

9. Press seam open.

10. With right sides together, join the BCD and BCA units with a ¼" seam.

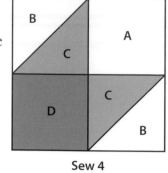

11. Press seam open. (This Four-Patch Variation Block should measure 8½" x 8½".)

Sew 4

## Back-Side Block

*The back-side block is a half-square log cabin design.*

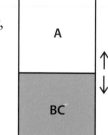

1. With right sides together, sew back-side square A to back-side square BC with a ¼" seam.

2. Press seam open.

3. With right sides together, sew back-side rectangle BCD to the BCA unit with a ¼" seam.

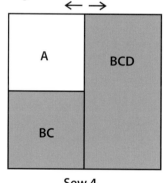

**Note:** If you're using a directional print, sew two BCD rectangles to left sides of BCA units and two BCD rectangles to right-hand sides of BCA units.

Sew 4

4. Press seam open.

## Quilting Instructions

Insert quilting needle size 90/14 into sewing machine. For best results, use a walking foot when quilting layers.

**Stitch suggestion:** Zigzag stitch 0.5 mm wide and 3.0 mm long (wobble stitch).

**Thread suggestion:** 50-weight cotton on top and in bobbin. Match thread to fabric for each side.

## Four-Patch Variation Block

1. Layer fabric and batting. With back-side block right side down, place batting in center, and place Four-Patch Variation Block right side up.

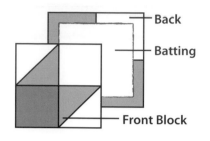

**Note:** Back-side block will be ¾" larger than front-side block on all sides.

2. Press layers together with steam.

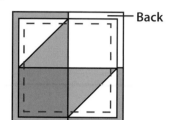

Dotted line indicates seam allowance, which is 1" from raw edges of back-side block.

**Note:** When using Cotton Theory Batting, pressing with steam will slightly melt the polyester in the batting and help fuse the layers together. Let the layers cool for a better bond before quilting.

3. Beginning in bottom left corner of block and using the wobble stitch, quilt to each of the three points and back again, pivoting at the starting point, as shown in diagram.

*Betty's Advice:*

*To create my favorite quilting stitch, the wobble stitch, set your zigzag at a very narrow width of 0.5 mm and stretch out the length to 3.0 mm.*

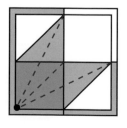

4. Quilt between these rows in same manner to create a total of seven rows.

5. Using a wobble stitch, quilt in the ditch, as indicated by zigzag in diagram.

6. Using edge of presser foot as a guide, quilt four additional rows, creating an echo effect.

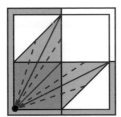
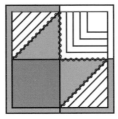

**Quilt 4**

## Leaves F and G

*You will be piecing and quilting at the same time.*

1. Layer fabric and batting. With back fabric right side down, place batting in center and place front fabric right side up.

2. Press layers together with steam.

3. Mark a diagonal line on the wrong side of square E.

**Note:** Two placemats will be mirror images of the others.

4. With right sides together, place square E on one end of rectangles F and G, as shown in diagram.

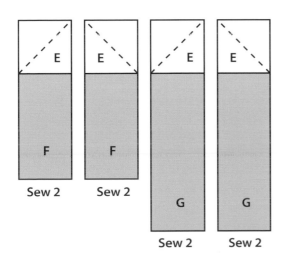

5. Using a wobble stitch, sew on the diagonal line, through all layers.

6. Trim square E and the front-side fabric ¼" from the stitching line, as shown in diagram. (Do not cut batting.)

7. Press triangles into corners, so right side of fabric is seen.

8. Using edge of presser foot as a guide, quilt four rows in the triangles, creating an echo effect.

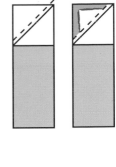

Trim

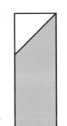

**Note:** Because the Cotton Theory 1" seam allowances will be folded and topstitched on the outside of the placemats, there should be no quilting within ¾" of the raw edges on the long sides of the rectangles.

9. Starting ¾" from raw edge of rectangle, as shown in diagram, quilt one presser-foot width away from seam line of triangle, and then pivot ¾" from other raw edge using needle down position. Sew about five stitches, pivot again and continue quilting rows in the same manner throughout the rectangle.

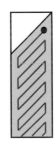

Quilt 2    Quilt 2
F and G   F and G

## Extension H

1. With back fabric right side down, layer batting even with one long edge of rectangle, and place front fabric right side up.

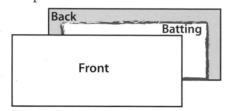

2. Press layers together with steam.

3. Place Adhesive Quilting Guide 1⅜" to right of sewing machine needle to provide a straight quilting row.

4. Quilt 1⅜" from long raw edge that has no batting in the seam allowance, as shown in diagram. (Quilt through entire length of rectangle.)

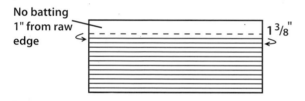

5. Using edge of presser foot as a guide, continue adding quilting rows across the rectangle, alternating directions to compensate for fabric shifting.

## Assembly Instructions

Insert topstitch needle size 90/14 into sewing machine.

Seam allowances will be finished on front side of placemats using the One-Way Street procedure, described in Techniques chapter.

**Note:** Use a 1" seam allowance when sewing your quilted pieces together.

**Thread suggestion:** 40-weight green variegated cotton on top and 50-weight red cotton in bobbin.

**Stitch suggestion:** Straight stitch 3.5 mm long; joining stitch 6.0 mm wide and 4.0 mm long.

## Four-Patch Block and Rectangle F

1. Rotate Four-Patch Variation Blocks so they appear as shown in diagram.

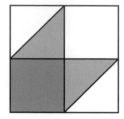 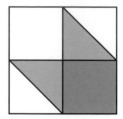

2. With back sides together (back fabrics against each other) and using a 1" seam, sew rectangle F to sides of Four-Patch Variation Block, as shown in diagram. Stitch through all fabric layers.

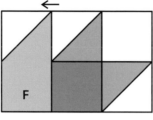 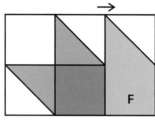

Construct 2        Construct 2

3. Press back side; then press all seam allowances on front side toward rectangle F.

4. Finish seams using the One-Way Street procedure, explained in Techniques chapter. (Trim one layer, fold two.)

5. With back sides together, sew rectangle G to the bottom edges of Four-Patch Variation Block with a 1" seam.

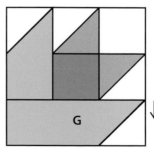 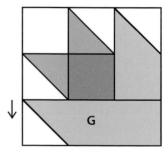

Construct 2        Construct 2

6. Press the back side; then press all seam allowances on front side toward rectangle G.

7. Finish seams using the One-Way Street procedure.

**Note:** The Four-Patch Variation Block is now a tulip block.

**Thread change:** Switch to 40-weight beige cotton on top.

8. With back sides together and using a 1" seam, sew long edge of Extension H that has no batting to the side of block, as shown in diagram.

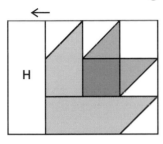

Construct 2        Construct 2

9. Press back side; then press all seam allowances on front side toward Extension H.

10. Finish seams using the One-Way Street procedure.

## Trimming

1. Trim ⅝" from raw edges on three sides of project, leaving a ⅜" seam allowance. (Extension H does not need to be trimmed.)

   Trimming is necessary before applying binding because the untrimmed placemat has no batting within 1" of raw edges on three of the sides.

## Applying Pocket

1. Fold down corner of pocket, and press with steam.

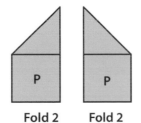

Fold 2        Fold 2

2. Place pocket on front side of Extension H, with bottom edges even and one side against the fold of the One-Way Street.

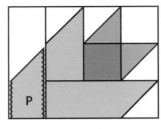

Topstitch 2        Topstitch 2

3. Topstitch sides of pocket in place, as shown in diagram, backstitching at top of pocket.

## Bias Binding

1. Apply binding to placemats. (See Bias Binding instructions near end of book.)

**Note:** When you put the four placemats relatively close together on a table, you will see a much larger design appear.

## Optional Napkins With Mitered Corners

1. Fold and press ¼" on all four sides of napkins.

2. Fold 1" and press again on all four sides.

3. Open a 1" corner (leave the ¼" pressed down), and fold the corner diagonally so that the pressed folds match up, as shown by arrows in diagram.

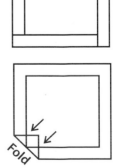

4. Press the diagonal corner fold.

5. Open the corner again (leave the ¼" pressed down).

6. With right sides together and edges even, fold through center of the corner, as indicated by dotted line in diagram.

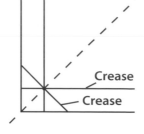

Crease
Crease

7. Sew on creased line created in Step 4, backstitching at beginning and end.

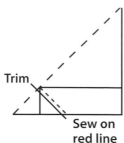

Trim

Sew on red line

8. Trim seam to ¼".

9. Press seam open.

10. Turn corner right side out, and press.

11. Finish remaining three corners in same manner, following steps 3 through 10.

12. Topstitch folded edges of napkin in place.

13. Fold napkin diagonally as desired, and insert in pocket of placemat.

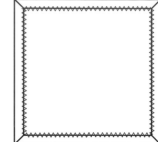

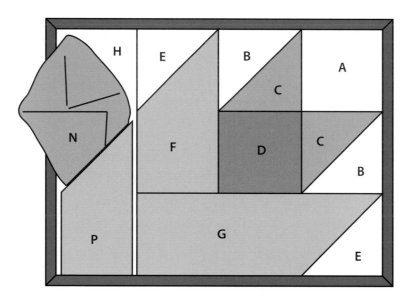

**Finished front side of Tulip Tango Placemat (set of four)**

*Two placemats will be mirror images of the others, with the napkin pocket on the right instead of the left.*

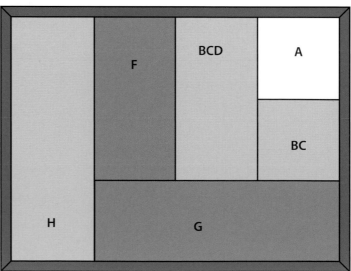

**Finished back side of Tulip Tango Placemat (set of four)**

*Two placemats will be mirror images of the others.*

# Triangle Twist Quilt

(93" x 104")

**Project features:**

- Framing strips
- Overpass™ procedure
- Highway™ procedure
- One-Way Street™ procedure

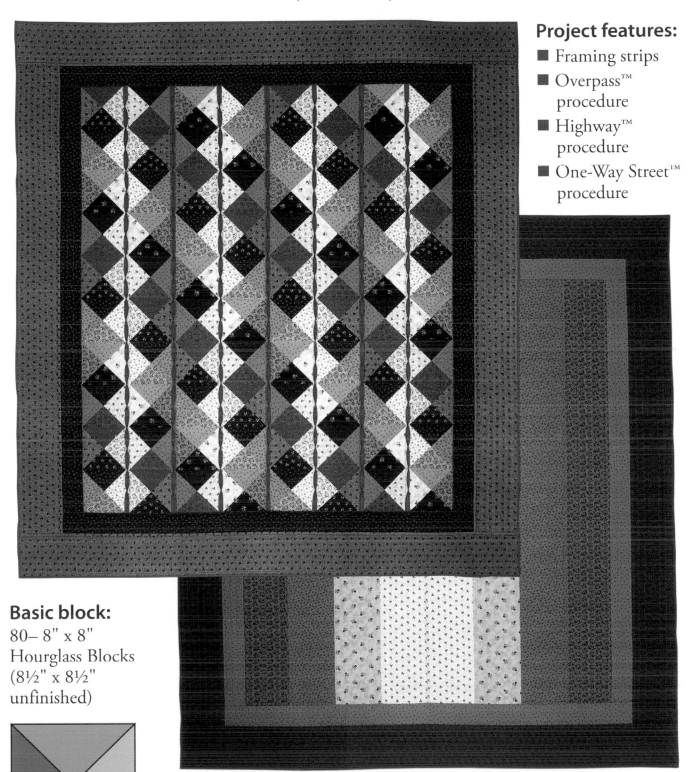

**Basic block:**
80– 8" x 8"
Hourglass Blocks
(8½" x 8½"
unfinished)

A unique technique called the Overpass™ procedure adds an eye-catching, red twist to this queen-size quilt. Wide stripes in shades of beige, tan, and brown adorn the back side of the reversible Triangle Twist Quilt.

## Yardage Requirements

*Based on 42-inch wide fabric*

### Front Side

*The quilt on the previous page was created using four different print fabrics for each A, B, C, D segment of the Hourglass Block. Yardage totals below are based on one print fabric per A, B, C, D. If you want to use additional prints, divide each yardage total accordingly.*

**Hourglass Blocks:**

**A:** 1½ yd. beige print

**B:** 1½ yd. blue-gray print

**C:** 1½ yd. brown print

**D:** 1½ yd. eggplant print

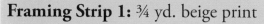

**Framing Strip 1:** ¾ yd. beige print

**Framing Strip 2:** ¾ yd. brown print

**Framing Strip 3:** 1¼ yd. red

**First Border:** 2½ yd. eggplant print

**Second Border:** 2¾ yd. brown print

### Back Side

**Rectangle 1:** 1¾ yd. dark brown print

**Rectangle 2:** 1¾ yd. brown print

**Rectangle 3:** 1¾ yd. tan print

**Rectangle 4:** 1¾ yd. beige print

**First Border:** 2½ yd. light blue-gray print

**Second Border:** 2¾ yd. dark blue-gray print

### Binding

⅞ yd. red

### Batting

Cotton Theory Batting, 18" x 16¼ yd.

## Fabric Cutting Instructions

Cut carefully to ensure you have an adequate amount of fabric. Label your cut pieces for each side of the project.

Where strips are listed, cut them on the crosswise grain (selvage to selvage); then cut sub-cuts from each strip on the lengthwise grain. (See diagrams in Preparation chapter for details.)

### Front Side

**Hourglass Blocks:**

**A (beige print):**
Cut 5– 9¼" strips
Sub-cut 20– 9¼" x 9¼"

**B (blue-gray print):**
Cut 5– 9¼" strips
Sub-cut 20– 9¼" x 9¼

**C (brown print):**
Cut 5– 9¼" strips
Sub-cut 20– 9¼" x 9¼"

**D (eggplant print):**
Cut 5– 9¼" strips
Sub-cut 20– 9¼" x 9¼"

**Framing Strip 1 (beige print):**

Cut 1– 20½" strip

Cut in half along fold, and piece together with ¼" seam to make 1– 40½" x 21" strip

Fold in half lengthwise, cut along fold again, and piece together with ¼" seam to make 1– 80½" x 10½" strip

Sub-cut 8– 1¼" x 80½"

**Framing Strip 2 (brown print):**

Cut 1– 20½" strip

Cut in half along fold, and piece together with ¼" seam to make 1– 40½" x 21" strip

Fold in half lengthwise, cut along fold again, and piece together with ¼" seam to make 1– 80½" x 10½" strip

Sub-cut 8– 1¼" x 80½"

**Framing Strip 3 (red):**
Cut 1– 41½" strip
Cut in half along fold, and piece together with ¼" seam to make 1– 82½" x 21" strip
Sub-cut 14– 1" x 82½"

**First Border (eggplant print):**
Cut 1– 82½" strip
Sub-cut 2– 6½" x 82½"
Sub-cut 2– 6½" x 79½"

**Second Border (brown print):**
Cut 1– 95½" strip
Sub-cut 2– 10½" x 95½"
Sub-cut 2– 10½" x 90½

## Back Side

### Rectangle 1 (dark brown print):
Cut 1– 56" strip
Sub-cut 3– 11" x 56"
Piece together with ¼" seam to make 1– 167" x 11" strip
Sub-cut 2– 11" x 82½"

### Rectangle 2 (brown print):
Cut 1– 56" strip
Sub-cut 3– 11" x 56"
Piece together with ¼" seam to make 1– 167" x 11" strip
Sub-cut 2– 11" x 82½"

### Rectangle 3 (tan print):
Cut 1– 56" strip
Sub-cut 3– 11" x 56"
Piece together with ¼" seam to make 1– 167" x 11" strip
Sub-cut 2– 11" x 82½"

### Rectangle 4 (beige print):
Cut 1– 56" strip
Sub-cut 3– 11" x 56"
Piece together with ¼" seam to make 1– 167" x 11" strip
Sub-cut 2– 11" x 82½"

### First Border (light blue-gray print):
Cut 1– 82½" strip
Sub-cut 2– 6½" x 82½"
Sub-cut 2– 6½" x 79½"

### Second Border (dark blue-gray print):
Cut 1– 95½" strip
Sub-cut 2– 10½" x 95½"
Sub-cut 2– 10½" x 90½"

## Binding
Cut 10– 2½" x 42" strips

## Batting Cutting Instructions

Cut longest pieces of batting first. Please label your cut pieces.

### Rectangles 1 through 4:
Cut 8  8" x 80"

### First Border:
Cut 2– 4" x 80"
Cut 2– 4" x 77"

### Second Border:
Cut 2– 8" x 93"
Cut 2– 8" x 88"

*See batting cutting diagrams on this page and next page.*

**Cutting diagram for Cotton Theory Batting (18" x 80")**
**Cut four of these, so you have a total of eight rectangles measuring 8" x 80".**
*(Gray area denotes batting that is not used.)*

137

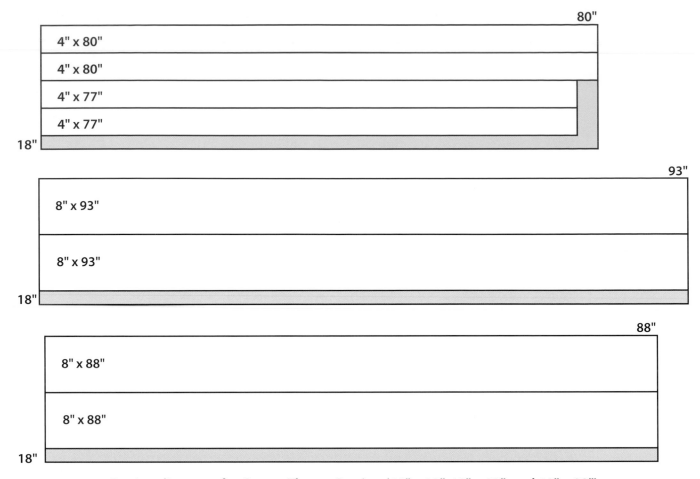

**Cutting diagrams for Cotton Theory Batting (18" x 80", 18" x 93", and 18" x 88")**

*(Gray area denotes batting that is not used)*

## Piecing Instructions

Insert a universal size 80/12 needle into sewing machine.

### Hourglass Block

1. Mark a diagonal line on wrong side of square A (9¼" x 9¼" beige print).

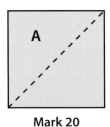

**Mark 20**

2. With right sides together, place square A on square B (9¼" x 9¼" blue-gray print).

3. Sew a ¼" seam on both sides of the diagonal line on square A, as shown in diagram.

**A**

**Sew 20**

4. Cut on diagonal line, and press seams open. (This will yield two half-square triangles.)

5. Mark a diagonal line on wrong side of square C (9¼" x 9¼" brown print).

6. With right sides together, place square C on square D (9¼" x 9¼" eggplant print).

7. Sew a ¼" seam on both sides of the diagonal line on square C.

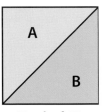

**Total of 40**

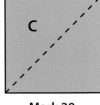

**Mark 20**

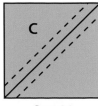

**Sew 20**

**138**

8. Cut on diagonal line, and press seams open. (This will yield two half-square triangles.)

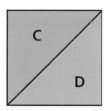

Total of 40

9. Mark a diagonal line on wrong side of square C/D, as shown in diagram.

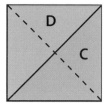

Mark 20

10. With right sides together, place square C/D on square A/B, with color A touching color D.

11. Sew a ¼" seam on both sides of diagonal line.

12. Cut on diagonal line, and press seams open. (This will yield two Hourglass Blocks. One will be the mirror image of the other.)

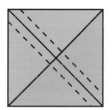

Sew 40

Block 1          Block 2

**Note:** You will have a total of 80 blocks, each measuring 8½" x 8½".

## Attaching Blocks Into Rows

1. With right sides together, match up colors, and sew Block 2 to Block 1 with a ¼" seam.

2. Press seam open.

3. Alternating Block 1 and Block 2, match up colors, and sew 10 blocks together to complete one row.

4. Press seams open.

5. Sew four rows, and label them Rows 1, 3, 5, and 7, as shown in next column.

6. Starting with Block 2, instead of Block 1, sew four more rows in same manner, matching colors and positioning blocks as shown in diagram.

7. Label them Rows 2, 4, 6, and 8.

## Framing Strip 1 and Framing Strip 2

1. With right sides together and using a ¼" seam, sew

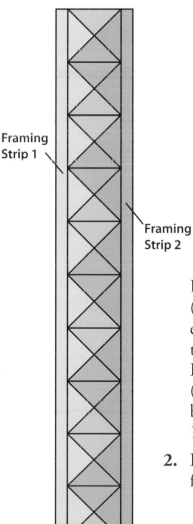

Framing Strip 1

Framing Strip 2

| | |
|---|---|
| Row 2 | Row 1 |
| Row 4 | Row 3 |
| Row 6 | Row 5 |
| Row 8 | Row 7 |

Framing Strip 1 (beige print) to beige edge of Rows 1 through 8, and sew Framing Strip 2 (brown print) to brown edge of Rows 1 through 8.

2. Press seams toward framing strips.

Sew framing strips to all 8 rows

## Quilting Instructions

Insert quilting needle size 90/14 into sewing machine. For best results, use a walking foot when quilting layers.

**Thread suggestion:** 50-weight tan cotton on top and in bobbin.

**Stitch suggestion:** Zigzag 0.5 mm wide and 3.0 mm long (wobble stitch).

### Rows 1 through 8

1. Arrange back-side Rectangles 1 through 4 in order and back again (1, 2, 3, 4, 4, 3, 2, 1).

2. Label the eight back-side rectangles as Rows 1 through 8.

   **Rectangle 1 – Row 1**
   **Rectangle 2 – Row 2**
   **Rectangle 3 – Row 3**
   **Rectangle 4 – Row 4**
   **Rectangle 4 – Row 5**
   **Rectangle 3 – Row 6**
   **Rectangle 2 – Row 7**
   **Rectangle 1 – Row 8**

3. Layer fabric and batting. Place back-side Rectangle 1 right side down, place batting in center, and place front-side Row 1 right side up.

**Note:** Back side will be ½" wider than front side on long edges and 1" longer than front side on short edges.

4. Press layers together with steam.

5. Pin layers together to secure them for quilting.

6. Layer the remaining rectangles and rows in same manner.

7. Press and pin layers.

8. Using wobble stitch (zigzag 0.5 mm wide and 3.0 mm long), quilt in the ditch on all diagonal seams, stitching to the raw edge of front-side fabric, as shown in left-hand diagram below.

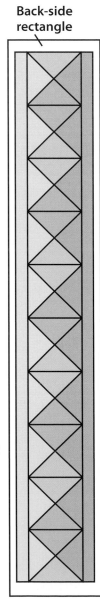

Back-side rectangle

**Layer 8 rows**

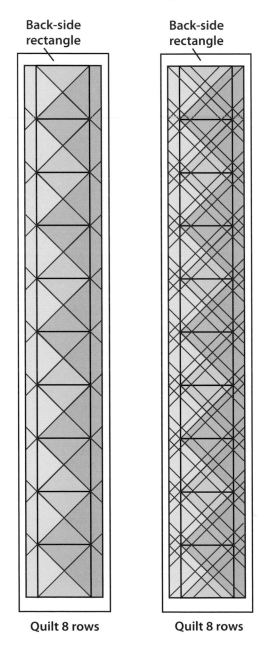

Back-side rectangle

Back-side rectangle

**Quilt 8 rows**    **Quilt 8 rows**

9. Quilt 1" away on boths sides of previous quilting, as shown in right-hand diagram above.

140

## Framing Strip 3

1. With right sides together and using a ¼" seam, sew Framing Strip 3 (red) to both long sides of Rows 2 through 7, lining up raw edges on front side of rows and stitching through all layers.

2. Press Framing Strip 3 toward outside of row so right side of fabric is visible.

**Note:** Raw edges of Framing Strip 3 will not be even with long edges of back-side fabric. Framing Strip 3 should hang about ¼" over both long edges.

3. Sew Framing Strip 3 to beige edge of Rows 1 and 8 in same manner as previous rows.

2. Press Framing Strip 3 toward outside of row so right side of fabric is visible.

## First Border

1. Layer back-side fabric right side down, batting in center, and front fabric right side up.

2. Press layers together with steam.

3. Place Adhesive Quilting Guide 1⅝" to right of sewing machine needle.

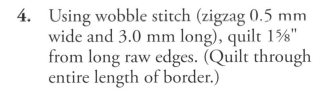

*Back-side fabric*

*Framing Strip 3*

*Sew to Rows 2 through 7*

4. Using wobble stitch (zigzag 0.5 mm wide and 3.0 mm long), quilt 1⅝" from long raw edges. (Quilt through entire length of border.)

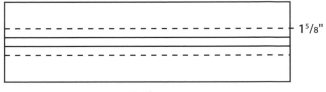

1⅝"

**Quilt 4**

5. Quilt two more rows toward the middle, 1" from previous quilting (total of four rows).

## Second Border

1. Repeat Steps 1 through 4 under First Border.

2. Quilt four more rows toward the middle, 1" apart, as shown in diagram.

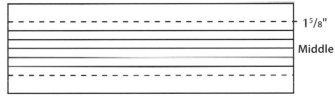

1⅝"

Middle

**Quilt 4**

3. Place Adhesive Quilting Guide 5¼" to right of sewing machine needle.

4. Quilt one row down the middle of each Second Border (total of seven rows).

## Assembly Instructions

Insert topstitch needle size 90/14 into sewing machine.

Seam allowances will be finished on front side of this project using the Highway™, One-Way Street™, and Overpass™ procedures, described in Techniques chapter.

**Important note:** Use a 1¼" seam allowance when sewing your quilted pieces together.

141

**Thread suggestion:** 50-weight red cotton on top and 50-weight tan cotton in bobbin.

**Stitch suggestion:** Straight stitch 3.5 mm long; joining stitch 6.0 mm wide and 4.0 mm long.

## Vertical Rows 1 through 8

1. With back sides together (back fabrics against each other) and using a 1¼" seam, sew Row 1 to Row 2, positioning rows as shown in diagram.

Row 1     Row 2

2. Press seam open on front side; then press back side.

3. Finish seam using the Highway procedure, explained in Techniques chapter.

**Note:** Your completed seam will be red, and Framing Strip 1 will be hidden beneath the folds.

4. Give your seam an extra lift with the Overpass procedure, explained in Techniques chapter. Pinch and pull up the folds of the Highway seam, and then bar tack the folds every 4 inches to make the seam three-dimensional.

**Close-up of Overpass procedure**

5. Sew together remaining Rows 2 through 8 in same manner, following Steps 1 through 4 and referring to diagram on next page for placement of rows. Fold and finish each seam before proceeding to the next row.

## First and Second Borders

1. With back sides together and using a 1¼" seam, sew First Border (6½" x 82½") to sides of quilt. as shown in diagram on next page.

2. Press the back side; then press all seam allowances on front side toward First Border.

3. Finish seams using the One-Way Street procedure, explained in Techniques chapter. (Trim one layer, fold two.)

4. With back sides together and using a 1¼" seam, sew First Border (6½" x 79½") to top and bottom of quilt.

5. Press seam allowances on front side toward First Border.

6. Finish seams using the One-Way Street procedure.

7. In same manner, sew Second Border (10½" x 95½") to sides of quilt and sew Second Border (10½" x 90½") to top and bottom of quilt. Finish with the One-Way Street procedure.

## Binding

1. Trim ⅝" from raw edges of quilt, leaving a ⅜" seam allowance on all sides.

2. Apply French-Fold Binding. (For instructions, see Binding chapter near end of this book.)

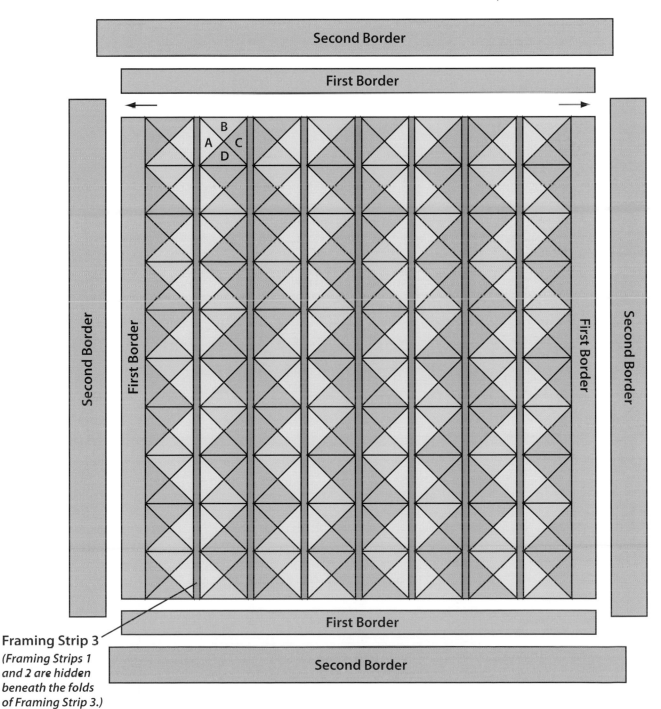

**Framing Strip 3**
*(Framing Strips 1 and 2 are hidden beneath the folds of Framing Strip 3.)*

# Jitterbug Rug

## (26" x 63")

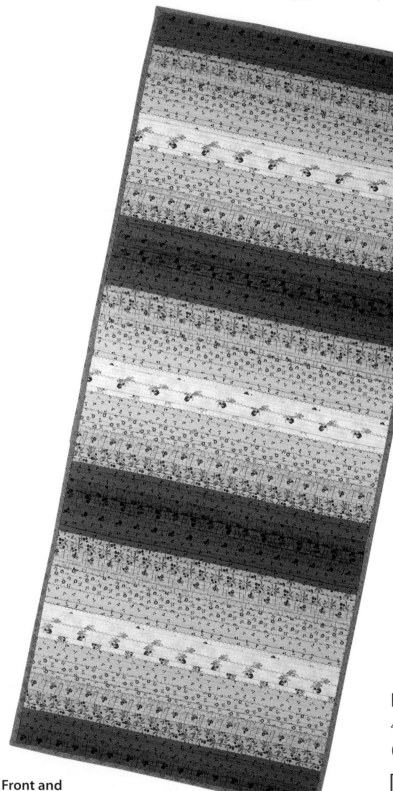

**Front and
back sides of this
Jitterbug Rug are made of the
same fabrics. This photo shows the front side.**

## Project features:

- Double batting
- Folded and topstitched seams on front side and back side
- Highway™ procedure

## Basic block:

42– 1½" x 26" rectangles
(3½" x 26" unfinished)

## Yardage Requirements

*Based on 42-inch wide fabric*

### Front Side and Back Side

*This yardage will be enough to construct both sides.*

### Rectangles 1 through 7:

¾ yd. each of seven assorted tan, beige, and brown prints

### Binding

⅜ yd. brown

### Batting

Cotton Theory Batting, 18" x 6 yd.
*Double batting is used in this project to make the rug stiffer.*

## Fabric Cutting Instructions

### Rectangles 1 through 7

**From each of seven assorted tan, beige, and brown prints:**

    Cut 1– 26" strip
    **For front side:** Sub-cut 6– 3½" x 26"
    **For back side:** Sub-cut 6– 3½" x 26"

### Binding

Cut 5– 3" x 42" strips

## Batting Cutting Instructions

Cut 84– 1½" x 26" (double batting)

## Quilting Instructions

Insert quilting needle size 90/14 into sewing machine. For best results, use a walking foot when quilting layers.

**Thread suggestion:** 40-weight brown variegated cotton on top and in bobbin.

**Stitch suggestion:** Zigzag 0.5 mm wide and 3.0 mm long (wobble stitch).

### Rectangles 1 through 7

1. Pair up like fabrics for front and back sides.

2. Layer fabric and batting. Place back fabric right side down, place two pieces of batting in middle (one on top of the other), and place front fabric right side up.

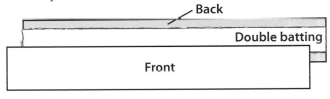

Layer 42

**Note:** Batting will extend all the way to short edges of rectangle, as shown in diagram.

3. Press layers together with steam.

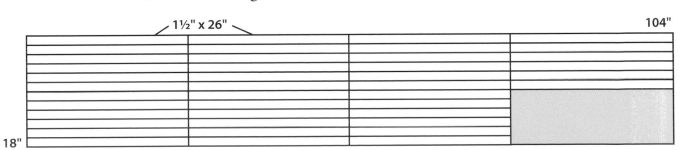

**Cutting diagram for Cotton Theory Batting (18" x 104")**
**Cut two of these, so you have a total of 84 rectangles measuring 1½" x 26".**
*(Gray area denotes batting that is not used.)*

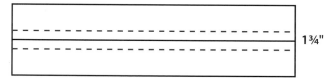

— 1¾"

4. Place Adhesive Quilting Guide 1¾" to right of sewing machine needle.

5. Quilt down the middle of each layered rectangle. (Quilt through the entire length of rectangles.)

6. Using edge of presser foot as a guide, quilt one more row on each side of the middle (total of three rows).

— 1¾"

**Quilt 42**

7. Arrange quilted Rectangles 1 through 7 from darkest to lightest colors.

8. Label rectangles using numbers 1 through 7, with 1 being the darkest fabric and 7 the lightest.

## Assembly Instructions

Insert topstitch needle size 90/14 into sewing machine.

Seam allowances will be 1" and will be finished on both sides of project using the Highway™ procedure, described in Techniques chapter.

**Stitch suggestion:** Straight stitch 3.5 mm long; joining stitch 6.0 mm wide and 4.0 mm long.

1. With **front** sides together (front fabrics against each other) and using a 1" seam, sew Rectangle 1 to Rectangle 2, stitching through all layers.

2. Press seam open on back side; then press the front side.

3. Fold and finish the seam allowances using the Highway procedure, explained in Techniques chapter.

**Note:** Finished seam allowances will alternate on the front side and back side, with the first seam finished on the back, the second on the front, the third on the back, the fourth on the front, etc.

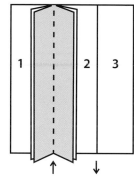

**Construct 6**

4. With **back** sides together (back fabrics against each other) and using a 1" seam, sew Rectangle 3 to Rectangle 2.

5. Press seam open on front side; then press the back side.

6. Finish seam using the Highway procedure.

7. With front sides together, sew Rectangle 4 to Rectangle 3.

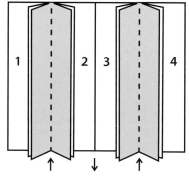

**Arrows indicate whether seam allowances are finished on the front side or back side.**

**Construct 6**

8. Press seam open on back side, and finish seam using the Highway procedure.

9. With back sides together, sew Rectangle 5 to Rectangle 4.

10. Press seam open on front side, and finish seam using the Highway procedure.

11. With front sides together, sew Rectangle 6 to Rectangle 5.

12. Press seam open on back side, and finish seam using the Highway procedure.

13. With back sides together, sew Rectangle 7 to Rectangle 6.

14. Press seam open on front side, and finish seam using the Highway procedure.

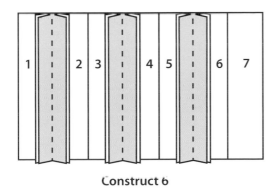

Construct 6

## Connecting the Sections

1. With front sides together, sew Rectangle 7 to another Rectangle 7, as shown in diagram in next column.

**Note:** Colors in the rug will go from dark to light and then light to dark.

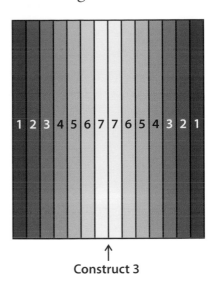

Construct 3

2. Press seam open on back side, and finish seam using the Highway procedure.

3. With back sides together, sew Rectangle 1 to another Rectangle 1 to join the three sections, as shown in diagram below.

4. Press seams open on front side, and finish seams using the Highway procedure.

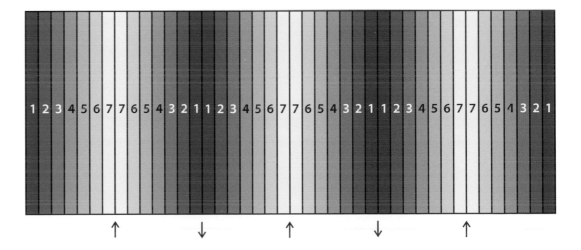

## Binding

1. Trim ½" from raw edges on short sides of rug.

2. Straighten up long sides of rug by trimming slightly, as needed.

3. Piece together ends of 3" binding strips with a mitered seam, and sew binding to rug with a ½" seam. (For instructions, see French-Fold Binding in the Binding chapter near end of this book, but use ½" seam and follow trimming instructions on this page in Steps 1 and 2.)

147

# Charleston Quilt
## (94" x 112")

Pieced connectors and machine embroidery add beautiful details to the star blocks of this reversible bed quilt. The front side is shown here. The back side is on the next page.

**Enlarged to show detail**

## Project features:

- Quilted embroidery
- Enlarged back-side blocks
- Pieced connectors
- Highway™ procedure
- One-Way Street™ procedure
- Freeway™ procedure
- Reversible binding

## Basic block:

20– 15" x 15" Star Blocks (15½" x 15½" unfinished)

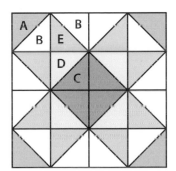

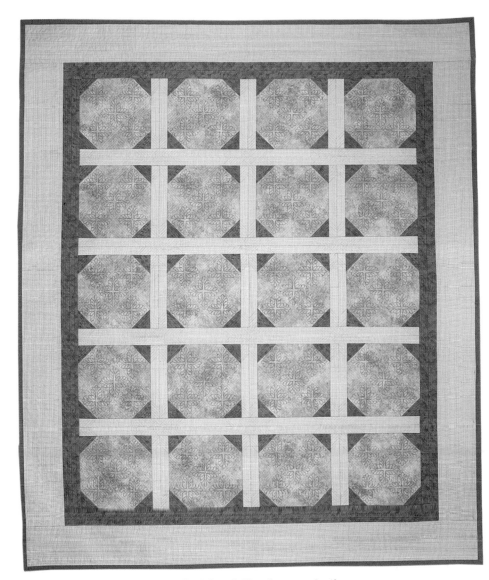

**Back side of Charleston Quilt**

## Yardage Requirements

*Based on 42-inch wide fabric*
*See block above and quilt diagram at end of this chapter for placement of pieces.*

### Front Side

**Star Blocks (Half-Square Triangles)**
  **A:** ¾ yd. eggplant
  **B:** 2 yd. beige
  **C:** ¾ yd. purple
  **D:** ¾ yd. sage green
  **E:** 1⅜ yd. olive green

**Short and Long Connectors**
**Rectangles 1 and 4:**
2 yd. olive green
**Rectangle 2:**
⅝ yd. eggplant
**Rectangle 3:**
2⅜ yd. beige
**First Borders 5 and 6:**
2¾ yd. eggplant
**Second Borders 7 and 8:**
2⅞ yd. eggplant/green print

### Back Side

**Back of Star Blocks:**
5 yd. sage green

**Half-Square Triangles:**
2½ yd. olive green
**Short and Long Connectors:**
3½ yd. green/beige check
**First Borders 5 and 6:**
2¾ yd. olive green
**Second Borders 7 and 8:**
2⅞ yd. green/beige check

### Reversible Binding

**Front side:** 1⅜ yd. eggplant
**Back side:** ¾ yd. olive green

### Batting

Cotton Theory Batting,
18" x 18¼ yd.

# Fabric Cutting Instructions

Cut carefully to ensure you have an adequate amount of fabric. Label your cut pieces for each side of the project.

Where strips are listed, cut them on the crosswise grain (selvage to selvage); then cut sub-cuts from each strip on the lengthwise grain. (See Preparation chapter for details.)

## Front Side

**Star Blocks (Half-Square Triangles):**
**A (eggplant):**
Cut 5– 4⅝" strips
Sub-cut 40– 4⅝" x 4⅝"
**B (beige):**
Cut 15– 4⅝" strips
Sub-cut 120– 4⅝" x 4⅝"
**C (purple):**
Cut 5– 4⅝" strips
Sub-cut 40– 4⅝" x 4⅝"
**D (sage green):**
Cut 5– 4⅝" strips
Sub-cut 40– 4⅝" x 4⅝"
**E (olive green):**
Cut 10– 4⅝" strips
Sub-cut 80– 4⅝" x 4⅝"

**Short and Long Connectors:**
**Rectangle 1 (olive green):**
Cut 5– 5¾" strips
Sub-cut 48– 3¾" x 5¾"
**Rectangle 2 (eggplant):**
Cut 3– 5¾" strips
Sub-cut 28– 3¾" x 5¾"
**Rectangle 3 (beige):**
Cut 6– 13¼" strips
Sub-cut 62– 3¾" x 13¼"
**Rectangle 4 (olive green):**
Cut 3– 13" strips
Sub-cut 24– 3¾" x 13"

**First Borders 5 and 6 (eggplant):**
Cut 1– 91" strip
**Border 5:** Sub-cut 4– 3¾" x 91"
**Border 6:** Sub-cut 4– 3¾" x 79½"

**Second Borders 7 and 8 (eggplant/green print):**
Cut 1– 98" strip
**Border 7:** Sub-cut 2– 10" x 98"
**Border 8:** Sub-cut 2– 10" x 95½"

## Back Side

**Back of Star Blocks (sage green):**
Cut 10– 17" strips
Sub-cut 20– 17" x 17"

**Half-Square Triangles (olive green):**
Cut 13– 6½" strips
Sub-cut 80– 6½" x 6½"

**Short and Long Connectors (green check):**
**Short:**
Cut 3– 17" strips
Sub-cut 30– 3¾" x 17"
**Long:**
Cut 1– 72½" strip
Sub-cut 8– 3¾" x 72½"

**First Borders 5 and 6 (olive green):**
Cut 1– 91" strip
**Border 5:** Sub-cut 4– 3¾" x 91"
**Border 6:** Sub-cut 4– 3¾" x 79½"

**Second Borders 7 and 8 (green/beige check):**
Cut 1– 98" strip
**Border 7:** Sub-cut 2– 10" x 98"
**Border 8:** Sub-cut 2– 10" x 95½"

## Reversible 1" Binding

**Front side (eggplant):**
Cut 11– 4¼" x 42" strips
**Back side (olive green):**
Cut 11– 2¼" x 42" strips

## Batting Cutting Instructions

Cut longest pieces first. Label your cut pieces.
**Blocks:** Cut 20– 15" x 15"
**Short Connectors:** Cut 30– 1¾" x 15"
**Long Connectors:** Cut 8– 1¾" x 70½"
**First Border 5:** Cut 4– 1¾" x 89"
**First Border 6:** Cut 4– 1¾" x 77½"
**Second Border 7:** Cut 2– 8" x 96"
**Second Border 8:** Cut 2– 8" x 93½"

*See diagrams on next page*

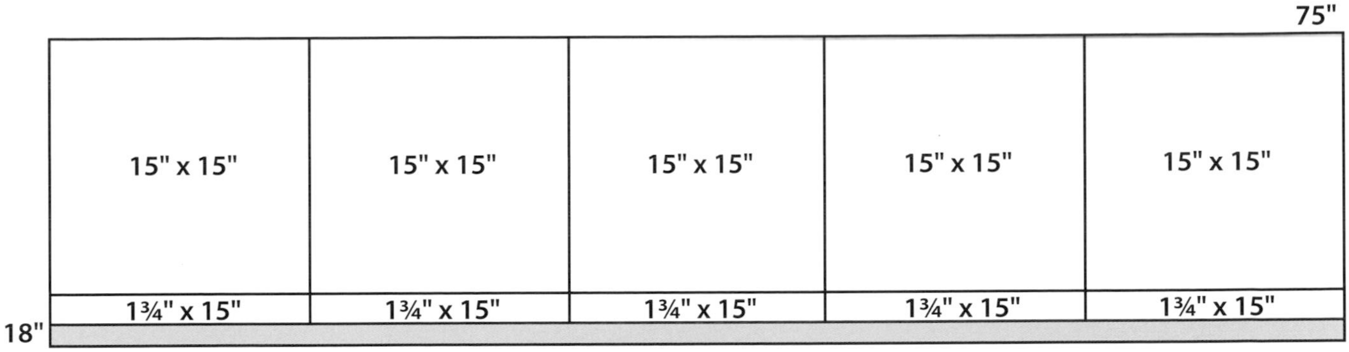

75"

| 15" x 15" | 15" x 15" | 15" x 15" | 15" x 15" | 15" x 15" |
| 1¾" x 15" | 1¾" x 15" | 1¾" x 15" | 1¾" x 15" | 1¾" x 15" |

18"

**Cut four of these, so you have a total of 20 rectangles measuring 15" x 15" and 1¾" x 15".**

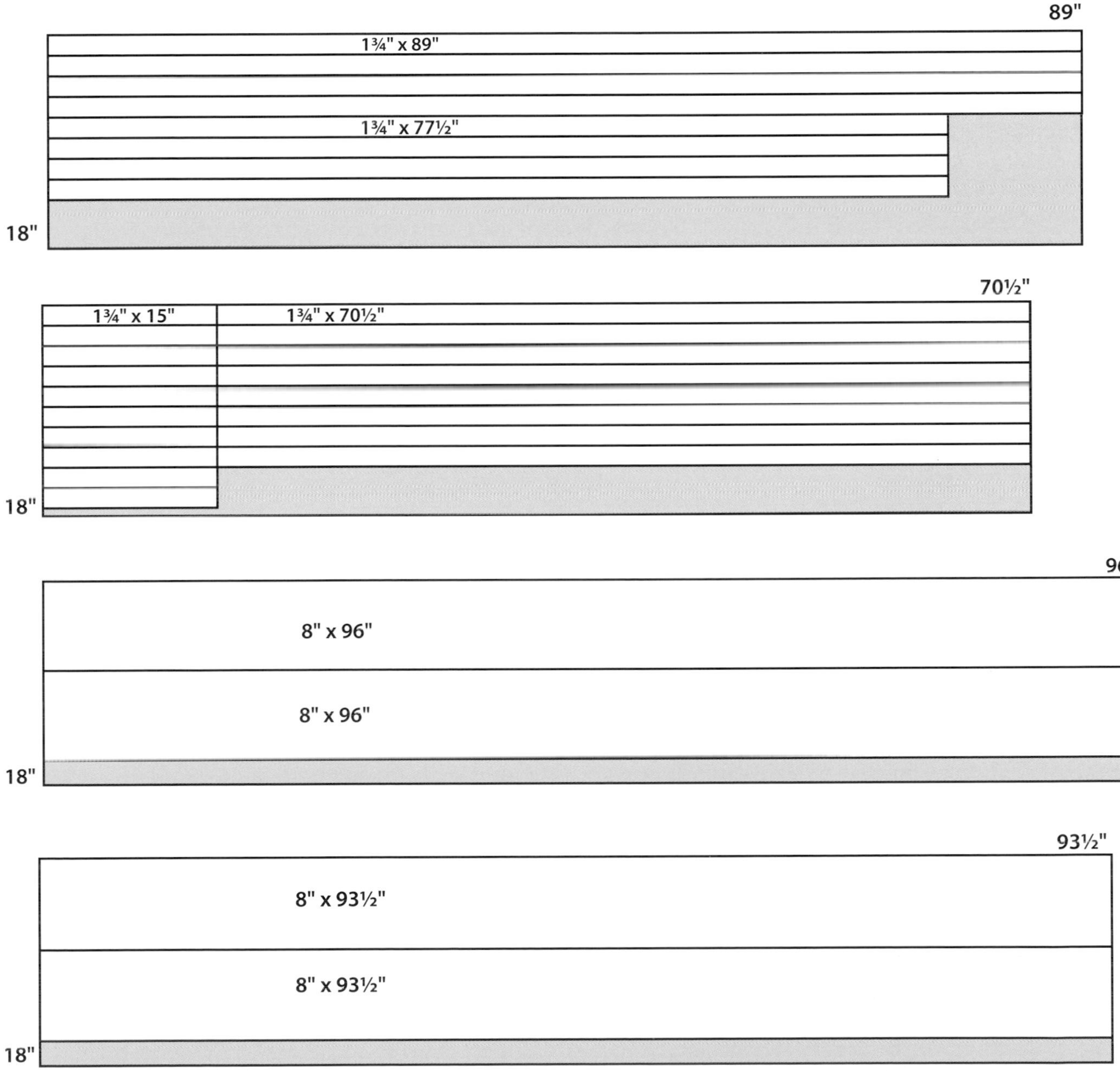

89"

1¾" x 89"

1¾" x 77½"

18"

70½"

1¾" x 15"    1¾" x 70½"

18"

96"

8" x 96"

8" x 96"

18"

93½"

8" x 93½"

8" x 93½"

18"

**Cutting diagrams for Cotton Theory Batting (18" x 75", 18" x 89", 18 x 70½, 18" x 96", and 18" x 93½")**

*(Gray area denotes batting that is not used)*

# Piecing Instructions

Insert universal needle size 80/12 into sewing machine.

## Star Block (15" x 15")

*This block is made up of 16 sets of half-square triangles.*

1. Mark a diagonal line on wrong side of squares B and D (4⅝" x 4⅝").

2. With right sides together, place square A (eggplant) on B (beige), place square C (purple) on D (sage green), and place square E (olive green) on B (beige).

3. Sew a ¼" seam on both sides of the diagonal line on squares B and D.

4. Cut on diagonal line. (This will yield two half-square triangles.)

5. Press seams open.

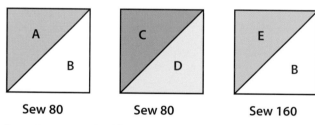

| Sew 80 | Sew 80 | Sew 160 |

6. Arrange half-square triangles in the order shown in diagram.

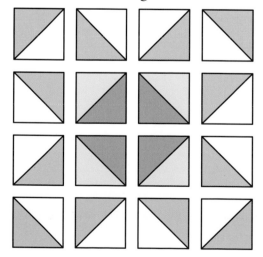

**Arrange 20 groups**

7. With right sides together, sew half-square triangles together into horizontal rows with a ¼" seam.

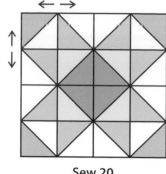

**Sew 20**

8. Press seams open.

9. Sew rows together with a ¼" seam.

10. Press seams open.

## Front-Side Short Connectors

**Note:** It is important to mark and sew diagonal lines accurately.

1. Mark a 45-degree diagonal line on wrong side of Rectangle 2, as shown in diagram. (Half of the marked rectangles will be mirror images of the others.)

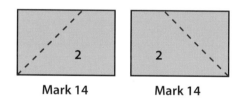

| Mark 14 | Mark 14 |

2. With right sides together, sew Rectangle 2 to Rectangle 3 on diagonal line (red dotted line in diagram), creating 12 total units.

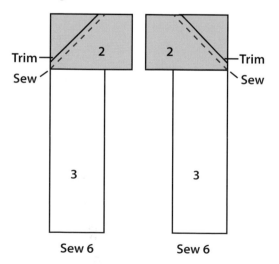

| Sew 6 | Sew 6 |

3. Trim excess fabric to ¼".

4. Press seam open.

**Note:** Remaining eggplant rectangles (Rectangle 2) will be added to Long Connectors later.

5. Mark a 45-degree diagonal line on wrong side of Rectangle 1. (Half of the marked rectangles should be mirror images of the others.)

6. With right sides together, sew Rectangle 1 to opposite end of Rectangle 3 on diagonal line (red dotted line in diagram), creating 12 Short Connectors. Pay close attention to the angle as you sew.

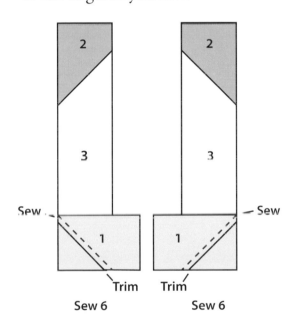

7. Trim excess fabric to ¼".

8. Press seam open.

9. With right sides together, sew Rectangle 1 to both ends of 18 additional Rectangle 3 on diagonal line (red dotted line in diagram).

10. Trim excess fabric to ¼".

11. Press seams open.

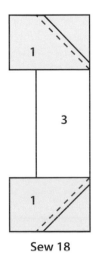

Sew 18

## Front-Side Long Connectors

1. With right sides together, sew one Rectangle 2 to one Rectangle 3 on diagonal line (red dotted line).

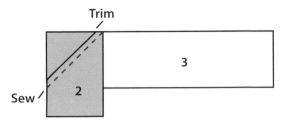

2. Trim excess fabric to ¼".

3. Press seam open.

4. Mark a 45-degree diagonal line on wrong side of Rectangle 4.

5. With right sides together, sew one Rectangle 4 to the previous Rectangle 3 on diagonal line (red dotted line).

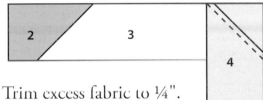

6. Trim excess fabric to ¼".

7. Press seam open.

8. Mark a 45-degree diagonal line on wrong side of another Rectangle 3.

9. With right sides together, sew one Rectangle 3 to the previous Rectangle 4, as shown in diagram below.

10. Trim excess fabric to ¼".

11. Press seam open.

12. Repeat Steps 5 through 11 two more times.

153

13. Then, with right sides together, sew one Rectangle 2 to the end of the row, as shown in diagram below.

14. Trim excess fabric to ¼".

15. Press seam open.

16. Make eight rows. Each row should measure 72½".

**Note:** Four rows will be turned upside down, giving you mirror-image rows.

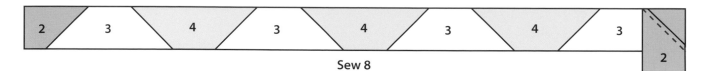

Sew 8

## Quilting Instructions

Insert quilting needle size 90/14 into sewing machine. For best results, use a walking foot when quilting layers.

### Star Blocks

**Suggested embroidery:** Square feather embroidery design Pfaff 394 Vintage Quilt Blocks, Pattern 7, stitch width 119.2 mm and length 119.0 mm. Design available through the Quilt Yard, Osseo, Wisconsin; phone (715) 597-2452 or (800) 673-8075.

**Thread suggestion:** 40-weight variegated green cotton on top and 50-weight sage green cotton in bobbin.

1. Layer fabric and batting. Place Back of Star Block (sage green) right side down, place batting in center, and place front-side Star Block right side up.

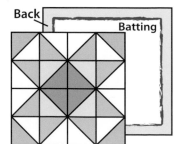

Back
Batting

**Note:** Back-side block will be larger than front.

2. Press layers together with steam.

3. Place all three layers in machine embroidery hoop, or follow alternate quilting instructions listed on next page.

**Note:** For machine embroidery, it may be helpful to put water-soluble stabilizer in embroidery hoop and then place the three quilt layers on top of stabilizer.

4. Size embroidery to fit area.

5. Embroider design five times, as shown in diagram.

Quilt 20 blocks

**Alternate quilting:** Quilt a simple star design, as shown in red in diagram.

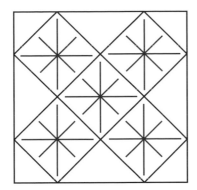

Red lines indicate quilting

## Additional Star Block Quilting

1. Using a wobble stitch (zigzag 0.5 mm wide and 3.0 mm long) and matching thread, quilt in the ditch in the triangle areas and around the center square, as shown in red in diagram.

Red lines indicate quilting in the ditch

2. Using edge of presser foot as a guide, echo quilt six rows in each area shown in diagram. (Do not quilt in the four corners of block.)

## Back-Side Half-Square Triangles

**Note:** Half-square triangles will be added to the corners of blocks on the back side, piecing and quilting at the same time.

1. With right sides together, place 6½" olive green squares in all four corners of back-side blocks.

2. Pin in place through all layers, as shown in diagram.

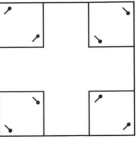

Back side of block

**Note:** You will be sewing diagonal lines from the front side of block and will not be able to see or remove pins while sewing, so place pins as indicated.

**Thread suggestion:** Match thread to the fabric for each side.

3. On front side of block, using wobble stitch (zigzag 0.5 mm wide and 3.0 mm long), quilt in the ditch diagonally across corners from raw edge to raw edge.

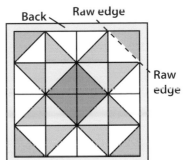

4. Press back-side triangles into corners.

**Note:** Back-side triangles may be larger than needed.

5. Trim overhanging portion so that back-side triangles are even with back of block.

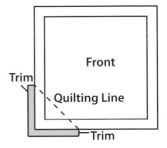

6. To remove excess layers on back of block, trim the back-side fabric and the second triangle layer (underneath the top triangle layer in each corner) to ¼" from the diagonal seam line. (Do not cut the top triangle layer, batting or front-side fabric.)

**Optional quilting:** To secure the Half-Square Triangles, use the edge of the presser foot as a guide, and channel quilt six rows in each corner, as shown in diagram. Match thread to the fabric for each side.

## Short Connectors

*There are 30 Short Connectors. A total of 18 have olive green pieces on each end, and 12 have eggplant on one end and olive green on the other.*

1. Layer back fabric right side down, batting in center, and front fabric right side up.

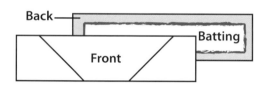

2. Press layers together with steam.

**Thread suggestion:** Match thread to the fabric for each side.

**Stitch suggestion:** Zigzag 0.5 mm wide and 3.0 mm long (wobble stitch).

3. Place Adhesive Quilting Guide 1⅜" to right of sewing machine needle to provide a straight quilting row.

4. Starting at diagonal seam line of each Short Connector, as shown in diagram, backstitch to secure quilting,

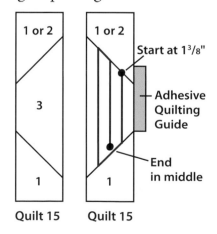

and quilt to opposite seam line. Pivot, stitch in the ditch about 11 or 12 stitches, pivot, quilt to the other seam line, pivot, stitch in the ditch about 5 or 6 stitches, pivot, and quilt down the middle, ending at the opposite seam line and backstitching.

**Note:** Sseam allowances of the Short Connectors will be folded on the outside of the quilt during assembly. Therefore, quilting lines should stop about ¾" from raw edges on the long sides.

5. Beginning in seam line, about ¾" from long raw edge, as shown in diagram, quilt in the ditch to about ¾" from opposite raw edge, pivot, and continue to quilt rows that are a presser-foot width away from the previous quilting (no need to backstitch).

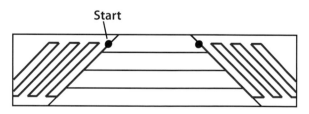

## Long Connectors

1. Layer back fabric right side down, batting in center, and front fabric right side up.

2. Press layers together with steam.

3. Quilt Rectangle 2 and Rectangle 3 in same manner as Short Connector, as shown in diagram at top of next page.

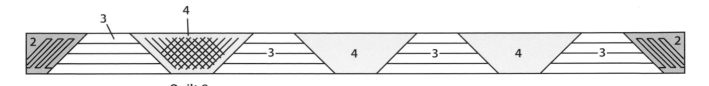

Quilt 8

**4.** Quilt Rectangle 4 diagonally in two directions, beginning in the seam line and staying about ¾" from raw edges on long sides of connector, as shown in diagram above. Providing the presser foot is ⅜" wide, quilt 10 rows in each direction.

## First Borders 5 and 6

**1.** Layer back-side fabric right side down, batting in center, and front fabric right side up.

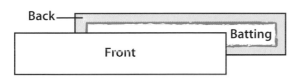

**2.** Press layers together with steam.

**3.** Place Adhesive Quilting Guide 1⅜" to right of sewing machine needle.

**4.** Using wobble stitch (zigzag 0.5 mm wide and 3.0 mm long), quilt 1⅜" from both raw edges. (Quilt through the entire length of borders.)

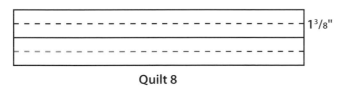

Quilt 8

**5.** Quilt one more row down the middle (total of three rows).

## Second Borders 7 and 8

**1.** Layer back-side fabric, batting, and front fabric, and press layers together with steam.

**2.** Secure layers with pins.

**3.** Place Adhesive Quilting Guide 5" to right of sewing machine needle.

**4.** Quilt down the middle of borders.

**5.** Using presser foot as a guide, quilt one row on each side of middle.

**6.** Place Adhesive Quilting Guide 1⅜" to right of sewing machine needle.

**7.** Quilt 1⅜" from long raw edges, as shown in diagram below.

**8.** Using presser foot as a guide along previous row, quilt two more rows toward the middle.

**9.** Measure the distance between groups of quilting rows.

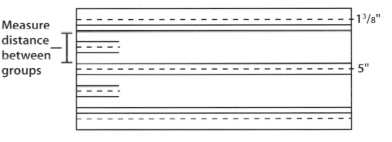

**10.** Find the center of this distance, and quilt one row in each open area.

**11.** Quilt one more row on each side of the previous quilting.

## Assembly Instructions

Insert topstitch needle size 90/14 into sewing machine.

Seam allowances will be finished on front side of this project using the One-Way Street™, Highway™, and Freeway procedures, described in Techniques chapter.

**Note:** Use a 1" seam allowance when sewing your quilted pieces together.

**Thread suggestion:** Green variegated 40-weight cotton on top and green 50-weight cotton in bobbin.

**Stitch suggestion:** Straight stitch 3.5 mm long; joining stitch 6.0 mm wide and 4.0 mm long.

## Star Blocks and Short Connectors

### Row 1, first block:

1. With back sides together and using a 1" seam, sew Short Connector unit 2-3-1 to right side of Star Block. Match up angles of seam lines, and stitch through all layers.

*Betty's Advice:* Use the Cotton Theory Adhesive Quilting Guide for accurate 1" seam allowances.

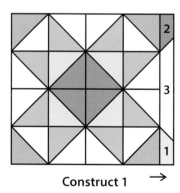

Construct 1 →

2. Press the back side; then press all seam allowances on front side toward Short Connector.

3. Finish seams using the One-Way Street procedure, explained in Techniques chapter. (Trim one layer, fold two.)

### Row 1, second and third blocks:

1. With back sides together, sew Short Connector unit 2-3-1 to both sides of Star Block, as shown in diagram at top of next column. Match up angles of seam lines.

2. Press the back side; then press seam allowances on front side toward Short Connectors.

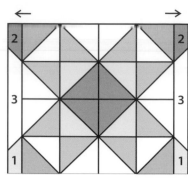

Construct 2

3. Finish seams using the One-Way Street procedure.

### Row 1, fourth block:

1. With back sides together, sew Short Connector unit 2-3-1 to left side of Star Block. Match up angles of seam lines.

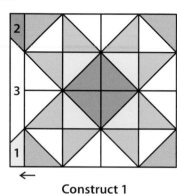

Construct 1

2. Press seam allowances on front side toward Short Connector.

3. Finish seams using the One-Way Street procedure.

### Rows 2, 3, and 4:

1. Construct in same manner as Row 1, using Short Connector 1-3-1 units.

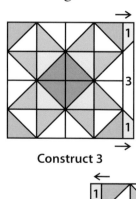

Construct 3

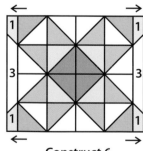

Construct 6

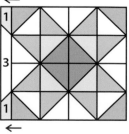

Construct 3

## Row 5:

1. Construct in same manner as Row 1, using Short Connector 1-3-2 units. (Rectangle 2 will be on the bottom of Row 5.)

## Connecting the Blocks

*Short Connectors will be sewn together and finished using the Highway procedure.*

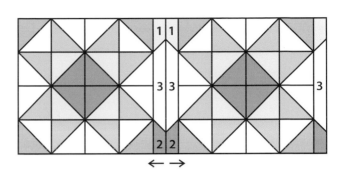

1. With back sides together and using a 1" seam, sew Short Connectors together.

2. Press seams open on front side; then press the back side.

3. Finish seams using the Highway procedure, explained in Techniques chapter.

4. Connect four blocks to complete each row.

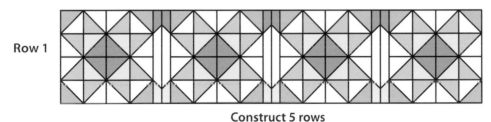

Row 1

**Construct 5 rows**

*Colors in Short Connectors will vary row by row. See quilt diagram on next page.*

## Connecting the Rows

*Long Connectors will be sewn to each row. Then the rows will be sewn together.*

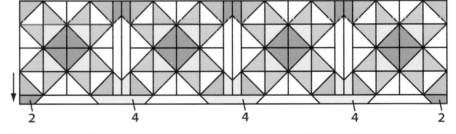

1. With back sides together and using a 1" seam, sew Long Connector to bottom of Row 1, to top and bottom of Rows 2, 3, and 4, and to top of Row 5, paying close attention to angle of seam lines.

2. Press the back side; then press all seam allowances on front side toward Long Connector.

3. Finish seams using the One-Way Street procedure.

4. With back sides together, sew Row 1 to Row 2.

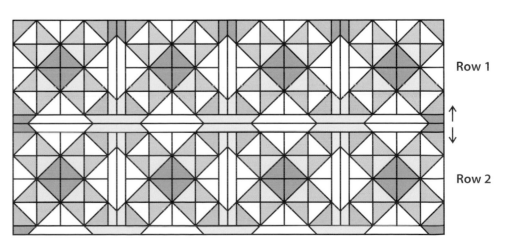

Row 1

Row 2

5. Press the back side; then press seams open on front side.

6. Finish seams using the Highway procedure.

7. With back sides together, sew Row 2 to Row 3, and finish seams using the Highway procedure.

8. Sew Row 3 to Row 4, and sew Row 4 to Row 5, finishing with the Highway procedure in the same manner.

## Completing the Borders

*An optional technique called the Freeway procedure was used to construct First Borders 5 and 6. The Freeway procedure is explained in the Techniques chapter. The Highway procedure can be used instead of the Freeway, if you prefer.*

1. With back sides together and using a 1" seam, sew two First Border 5 pieces together, as shown in diagram below.

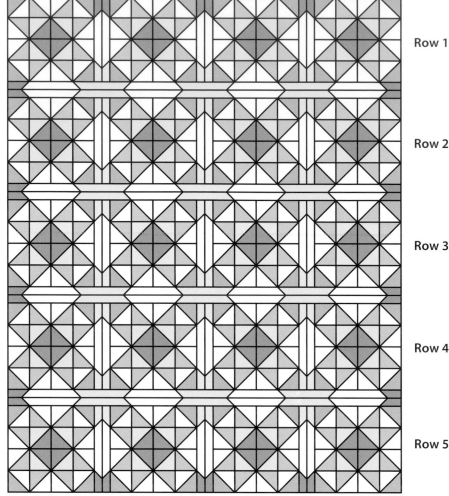

Row 1

Row 2

Row 3

Row 4

Row 5

| 5 |
|---|
| 5 |

2. Press seam open on front side; then press the back side.

**Note:** To use the Freeway procedure, your back-side fabric must coordinate with the front-side fabric. View fabric colors while seam is pressed open. If you do not like the back-side fabric showing on the front side, use the Highway procedure instead of the Freeway to finish the seam.

3. Finish seam using Freeway procedure, explained in Techniques chapter.

4. Repeat steps 1 through 3 for remaining First Border 5 pieces and for First Border 6.

5. With back sides together and using a 1" seam, sew First Border 5 to sides of quilt, as shown in diagram on next page.

6. Press all seams on front side toward First Border 5, and finish with the One-Way Street procedure.

7. With back sides together, sew First Border 6 to top and bottom of quilt, and finish with the One-Way Street procedure.

8. Sew Second Border 7 to sides of quilt and Second Border 8 to top and bottom of quilt in the same manner, and finish with the One-Way Street procedure.

## Binding

1. Binding will finish with a 1" seam. There is no need for trimming before binding is applied.

2. Apply Reversible Binding. (For instructions, see Binding chapter near end of this book, but do not trim project.)

# Part Four
# Finishing Up

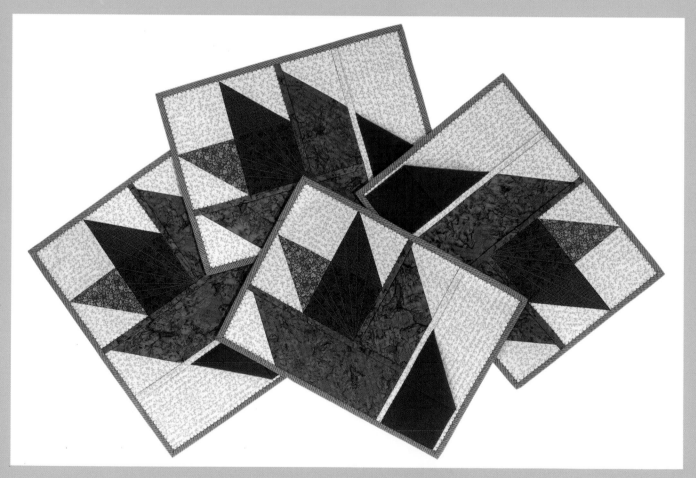

**Bias binding adds the perfect finishing touch
to these Tulip Tango Placemats.**

# Binding

## French-Fold Binding

Machine-applied French-fold binding is the easiest type of binding to use to finish your quilt, and it adds durability to the quilt's edges.

**Note:** Binding strips usually are 2½" wide.

Before adding binding, trim ⅝" from the raw edges of your project, leaving a ⅜" seam allowance on all sides. Trimming is necessary because Cotton Theory projects have no batting within 1" of raw edges.

1. With right sides together, piece together binding strips with mitered seams (45-degree angle), as shown in diagram.

2. Stitch a diagonal line across the two strips.

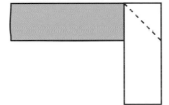

3. Trim the excess to ¼".

4. Press the seam open so binding lies flat.

## The Magic Triangle:

The Magic Triangle will help you make a mitered seam when stitching the beginning and ending binding tails together.

1. With wrong side facing up, fold down left end of binding to form a triangle and press with steam iron.

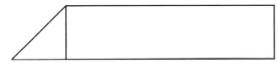

2. With wrong sides together, fold binding in half lengthwise and press, as shown in diagram at top of next column.

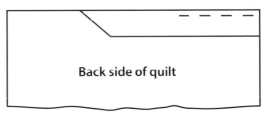

## Applying Binding to Quilt:

**Note:** Binding will be sewn to the back side of project, then folded to the front side and machine-stitched into place.

1. With raw edges even, sew binding to back of quilt with a ⅜" seam, beginning in the middle of one side and leaving the first 6" of binding free of stitching.

Back side of quilt

2. Stop stitching ⅜" from the corner and backstitch.

3. Remove quilt from sewing machine.

4. Fold binding up, creating a 45-degree angle, and press with fingers.

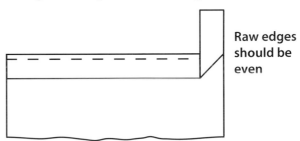

Raw edges should be even

5. Fold binding straight down, with the folded edge of the binding even with the quilt edge (45-degree angle will be hidden.)

6. Using a ⅜" seam, begin stitching at the fold and backstitch.

Folded edge

7. Continue applying binding in this manner around all corners.

8. Stop sewing about 6" from starting point, leaving the last 6" of binding free of stitching.

9. Tuck the ending binding tail inside the beginning binding tail, where the Magic Triangle is pressed in place. Open up binding.

**Cut ending binding tail**

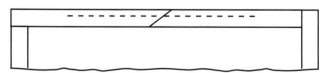

10. Cut ending binding tail even with right-hand side of Magic Triangle.

11. Pin ending binding tail to Magic Triangle, matching top and side edges.

12. Sew together at 45-degree angle on creased, diagonal line of Magic Triangle.

13. Trim the excess to ¼", and press seam open.

14. Refold binding in half.

15. Stitch the remaining seam.

16. Press binding flat toward the outside.

## Machine-Stitching Binding in Place

**Note:** Fold top binding first; then fold the left side binding.

1. Fold top binding to front side, back to the original seam. Finger-press folded binding at corner, forming a 45-degree angle.

**Front side of quilt**

**Note:** It may be necessary to hand tack binding in corners. You will be using a decorative stitch or zigzag to secure binding.

2. Fold left side binding to front side, back to the original seam. (Fold bottom and right-hand side in same manner.)

3. With a decorative stitch of your choice, stitch in the ditch (on the original seam) to sew binding into place.

## Bias Binding

Trim raw edges of quilt before applying binding. Refer to each project's instructions for details on trimming.

Fabrics such as checks and plaids, become more attractive when cut on the bias.

### Cutting Instructions:

Remove selvages. A ⅝-yard strip of fabric will yield two 21" squares.

1. Cut a 21" x 21" square.

2. Fold in half diagonally (do not press the fold).

3. Place fold on a horizontal grid line on cutting mat.

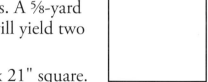

**Fold**

4. Place tip of triangle on a vertical grid line on cutting mat.

5. Cut binding strips at the width required for your project.

**Note:** These binding strips will have mitered ends ready to sew together.

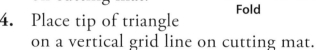

**Fold**

6. With right sides together, sew bias strips end to end with a ¼" seam.

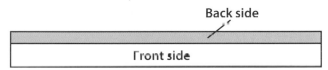

7. Press seams open.

8. Refer to French-Fold Binding in this chapter for instructions on applying binding to quilt.

## Reversible Binding

When constructing reversible quilts, you may not have a compatible binding fabric for both sides of the project. Reversible binding consists of two fabrics sewn together so the fabrics coordinate with each side.

**Note:** Binding strips usually are cut 2¼" wide for the front side and 1¼" wide for the back, but this can vary, depending on how wide you want the finished binding to be. The Charleston Quilt in this book, for instance, has front-side binding strips that are 4¼" wide, and back-side strips that are 2¼" wide.

Before adding binding, trim ½" from the raw edges of your project, leaving a ½" seam allowance on all sides. Trimming is necessary because Cotton Theory projects have no batting within 1" of the raw edges.

1. With right sides together, piece together front-side binding strips with mitered seams (45-degree angle), as shown at top of next column.

The Charleston Quilt features reversible binding — green on one side and eggplant on the other.

2. Stitch a diagonal line across the two strips.

3. Trim the excess to ¼".

4. Press the seam open.

5. With right sides together, piece together back-side binding strips with mitered seams. Repeat Steps 2 through 4.

### Joining Front-Side and Back-Side Binding:

1. With right sides together, sew front-side binding to back-side binding lengthwise with a ¼" seam and a short stitch length (2.0 mm).

2. Set the seam by pressing the stitching.

3. Press seam open.

Back side

Front side

### The Magic Triangle:

The Magic Triangle will help you make a mitered seam when stitching the beginning and ending binding tails together.

1. With wrong side facing up, fold down left end of binding to form a triangle and press.

Wrong side

2. With wrong sides together, fold binding in half lengthwise and press.

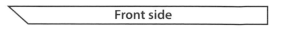

Front side

### Applying Binding to Quilt:

**Note:** Binding will be sewn to the back side of project and then folded to the front side.

1. With raw edges even and seam at bottom of binding, sew both layers of binding to back side of quilt with a ½" seam, beginning in center on one side and leaving first 6" free of stitching.

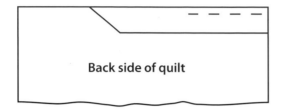

**Back side of quilt**

2. Stop stitching ½" from the corner, and then backstitch.

3. Remove quilt from sewing machine.

4. Fold binding up, making a 45-degree angle, and press with fingers.

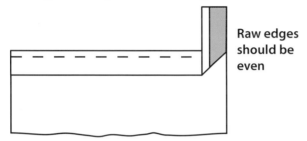

Raw edges should be even

5. Fold binding straight down, with the folded edge of the binding even with the quilt edge (45-degree angle will be hidden.)

6. Using a ½" seam, begin stitching at the fold and backstitch.

Folded edge

7. Continue applying binding in this manner around all corners.

8. Stop sewing 6" from the start, leaving last 6" of binding free of stitching.

9. Tuck the ending binding tail inside the beginning binding tail, where Magic Triangle is located. Open up binding.

**Cut ending binding tail**

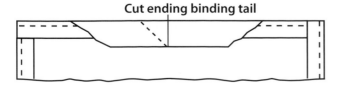

10. Cut ending binding tail even with right-hand side of Magic Triangle.

11. Pin ending binding tail to Magic Triangle, matching top and side edges.

12. Sew together at 45-degree angle on creased, diagonal line of Magic Triangle.

13. Trim excess to ¼" and press seam open.

14. Refold binding in half.

15. Stitch the remaining seam.

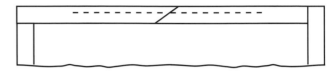

16. Press binding flat toward the outside.

## Machine-Stitching Binding in Place:

**Note:** You will see the reversible binding starting to take effect. Fold top binding first; then fold left side binding.

1. Fold top binding to front side, back to original seam. Finger-press folded binding at corner, forming a 45-degree angle.

**Front side of quilt**

**Note:** It may be necessary to hand tack binding in corners. You will be using a zigzag or decorative stitch to secure binding in place.

2. Fold side binding to front side, back to original seam. (Remaining binding should be folded in same manner as Steps 1 and 2.)

3. With a decorative stitch of your choice, stitch in the ditch (on the original seam) to sew binding into place.

## About the Author

Betty Cotton is a quilting entrepreneur, teacher, fabric designer, and author. She invented Cotton Theory quilting in 2001 and received a patent on it in 2004. Her first book, *Cotton Theory Quilting: Quilt First–Then Assemble,* was published in 2006. She owns a quilt shop and retreat center in Osseo, Wisconsin.

## Join Betty at Cotton Theory Camp

Learn basic and advanced techniques of Cotton Theory quilting at a five-day training camp. Betty Cotton teaches Cotton Theory Camp several times a year in Osseo, Wis. Dates and details are available on the Internet at www.quiltyard.com.

# Special Thanks

**A special thank you to the certified Cotton Theory instructors who donated their time to make several large quilts in a short period of time:**

Nancy Eichel

**Nancy Eichel, Dryden, Ontario** – "I thoroughly enjoyed the entire process of creating Nine-Patch Polka. The connectors add an eye-catching third dimension to the blocks, and the sashing forms a floating star in the intersections, giving my quilt so much drama."

**Donna Hanson, Eau Claire, Wis.** – "Feathered Fling was constructed as a team effort with my mother **(Loretta Jarocki of Withee, Wis.),** who hand-embroidered all 50 state birds in just 87 days, and myself, who quilted and joined the blocks together. Using Betty Cotton's theory added the perfect amount of detail and dimension to each of the blocks and accentuated the embroidery wonderfully!"

Photo by Ann DeBruyckere

Loretta Jarocki
and Donna Hanson

**Betty Nyseth, Cumberland, Wis.** – "Cotton Theory allowed me to machine quilt American Promenade in small sections and then sew my pieces together. Many words describe Betty Cotton's method: Unique, creative, addicting, dimensional, reversible, inspirational!"

Betty Nyseth

**Sue Wilson, Huron, Ohio** – "After many years of traditional quilting, Cotton Theory has revitalized me as a quiltmaker. I loved piecing the blocks for Log Cabin Shuffle, but loved even more having this quilt completed without traditional quilting!"

Sue Wilson and Betty Slezak

**Betty Slezak, Huron, Ohio** – "The squares in my quilt, Ohio Reel, sat on my shelf over a year. Betty Cotton helped me use decorative stitches and embroidery to make them beautiful."

**Katie Wolff, Osseo, Wis.** – "As Betty Cotton's daughter, quilting has been part of my life from the beginning. It's fun to be creative with the quilting, especially when it's manageable. The pieced rows in Triangle Twist allowed me to play with the design of the quilting."

Katie Wolff

# Ordering Information

## Supplies

### Cotton Theory products
Adhesive Quilting Guide
Cotton Theory Batting
Cotton Theory Scissors
*Cotton Theory Quilting: Quilt First – Then Assemble (Book One)*
*Cotton Theory Quilting 2: Traditional Blocks (Book Two)*
Cotton Theory pattern booklets
Cotton Theory instructional DVD
Betty Cotton's Cottage Colors 12-spool set of King Tut 40-weight variegated cotton thread

### Anita Goodesigns
Feather embroidery designs, Quilt Feathers Pattern 12 and Quilt Feathers Mini Collection Pattern 23C

### Cactus Punch Embroidery
Snowflake 4 and Snowflake 1, Vol. 45, Adventures In Fleece

### Pfaff Embroidery
Square feather embroidery design, Pfaff 394 Vintage Quilt Blocks, Pattern 7

### Colonial Patterns, Inc.
Aunt Martha's Hot Iron Transfers, Design 626, State Birds

### Ackfeld Manufacturing
Classic Motifs 22" Flower Garden quilt hanger

### Anazazi
Fingering-weight variegated alpaca yarn

### Hera marker

### OESD, Inc. Embroidery
Left Foot Print NV258
Right Foot Print NV257

## Where to Order

**Cotton Theory® LLC**
**13900 7th Street, PO Box 22**
**Osseo, WI 54758**
**Phone:** (715) 597-2883 or (800) 673-8075
**E-mail:** sales@quiltyard.com
**Internet:** www.quiltyard.com

**Quilt Yard® LLC**
**13900 7th Street, PO Box 277**
**Osseo, WI 54758**
**Phone:** (715) 597-2452 or (800) 673-8075
**E-mail:** sales@quiltyard.com

**Oklahoma Embroidery Supply & Design, Inc.**
**www.EmbroideryOnline.com**